INSIGHT COMPACT G

POLAND

Compact Guide: Poland is the ideal quick-reference guide to this fascinating country. It tells you all you need to know about Poland's attractions, from the splendours of Warsaw, Cracow and Gdansk to the serenity of Masuria, the drama of Dunajec Gorge and the grandeur of the Tatra Mountains.

This is just one title in *Apa Publications'* new series of pocket-sized, easy-to-use guidebooks intended for the independent-minded traveller. *Compact Guides* pride themselves on being up-to-date and authoritative. They mini travel encyclopedias, designed to be comprehensive yet portable, both readable and reliable.

Star Attractions

An instant reference to some of Poland's most popular tourist attractions to help you on your way.

Monument to the Warsaw Uprising p19

The Barbican p20

Radziwill Palace p21

Lazienki Palace p23

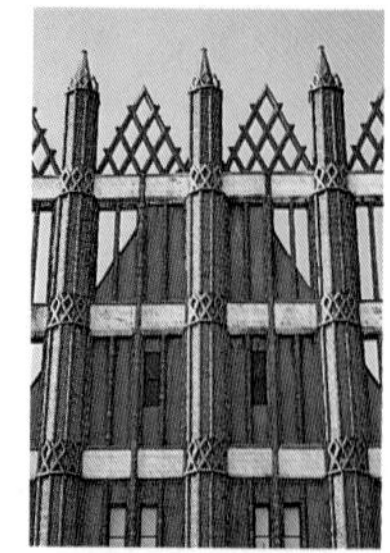

Szczecin's Old Town Hall p26

Long Market, Gdansk p33

Malbork Castle p39

Open-air museum p41

Biskupin p52

Rafting on the Dunajec p60

Copernicus p4

Poland

Introduction

Places

Culture

Leisure

Practical Information

Poland – Cities, Scenery and Solidarity

Opposite: Sigismund Chapel, Cracow

Mountains, forests, sandy beaches, culture and history – Poland's got them all and is growing more and more popular as a holiday destination. Since the victory of the Solidarity trade union movement transformed life in Poland by throwing open doors to the West, tourists have been embarking on adventures of discovery in a country that has many diverse activities on offer.

Through a thousand years of dramatic history when Poland was constantly being fought over and divided up by neighbours, the Poles have become masters of reconstruction and renovation. As invaders came and went some left an inheritance of magnificent architecture while others razed towns to the ground. Today there is little to show of the great destruction the country suffered in World War II, as towns and cities have been masterfully and lovingly restored. Gdansk, Cracow and Warsaw compete in presenting the most magnificent Old Town.

Although in some parts a legacy of pollution has been left by the old regime, there is plenty of unspoilt countryside for nature lovers and those in search of outdoor relaxation. Long, lonely sandy beaches edge the Baltic Sea, and Masuria – the land of a thousand lakes – is teeming with wildlife. The magnificent alpine peaks in the southeast contrast with the widespread lowlands that roll seductively into the dark pine forests. Unusual and original scenery has been preserved in national parks, which also offer a final refuge to many rare animals such as the European bison.

Baltic beaches

Canoeing in Masuria

With such a diverse landscape, Poland is a paradise for those who enjoy an active holiday, whether it be hiking, climbing or skiing in the mountains, or fishing, sailing or canoeing in the vast network of lakes and rivers.

Hospitality is a tradition in this country, where poverty is forgotten when there are guests and around every corner a warm welcome awaits visitors. Tables groan with food and this is reflected in the hotels, restaurants and guesthouses that are mushrooming under private ownership.

The Poles love an excuse for a feast and the country is steeped in folklore, providing scope for colourful festivals in the summer, when the national costume is aired. Despite the centuries of foreign rulers, the Poles have held on to their identity and remained patriotic throughout as has been shown by their famous sons.

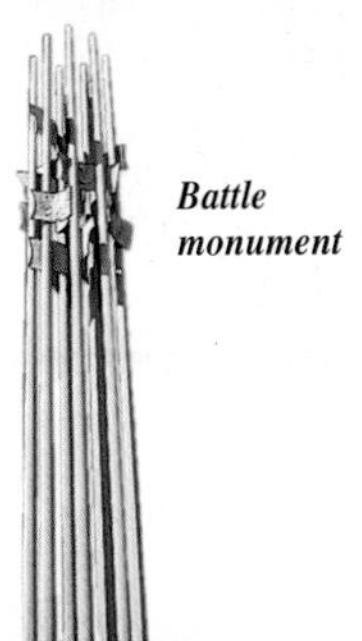

Battle monument

Polish-born Frederic Chopin spent his adult years away from his native land, but the composer never forgot his home in his work and every year is honoured in music festivals across the country.

Poland is a bridge between two great cultural spheres and visitors will experience a mixture of the unusual and the familiar as they travel. Of course, its infrastructure has not yet reached the standards of the West, but with a little patience and understanding almost every situation can be mastered.

Position and landscape

Although many people still think of Poland as being part of Central Europe, from a geographical point of view the opposite is the case: Poland is situated many hundreds of kilometres west of the geographical centre of Europe, which is actually in Lithuania.

Today the national territory of Poland extends from the Baltic in the north to the Carpathians in the south, from the River Bug in the east to the Odra in the west, covering a total area of 312,683sq km (120,727 sq miles), which roughly corresponds to the UK and Ireland put together or half the area of Texas. It is bordered by the countries of Germany, the Czech Republic, Slovakia, the Ukraine, Belorussia, Lithuania and the Russian Federation (Kaliningrad region), and has a total of exactly 3,538km (2,199 miles) of national border.

Rural tranquillity

Life in the slow lane

Poland is primarily flat with two-thirds of the country rising no more than 200m (656ft) above sea level. The lakes in the north were formed by glaciers during the Ice Age. The adjoining central Polish lowlands are mainly agricultural and the plateaux to the south are the remains of ancient mountain ranges that have been worn away over millions of years. The Carpathian and Sudety Mountains form Poland's southern boundary with the highest summit in the country, the Rysy (2,499m/8,199ft), located in the Tatra Mountains, the highest range in the Carpathians.

Climate and when to visit

Poland's climate is classified by meteorologists as temperate – a description frequently disputed by both the country's inhabitants and its visitors. This is because Poland is located in a transition zone between the Western European maritime climate and the Eastern European continental climate, which makes the weather extremely changeable. The seasons do not necessarily coincide with the calendar either, and can differ considerably from year to year, so that the following description of the country's climate is only a rough indication of what to expect. Spring is sunny and warm, but there are sometimes heavy frosts at night, even in May. In summer, from June to August, temperatures often reach 30°C (86°F); most of the rain falls in the mountains where thunderstorms are frequent. On the other hand, the weather on the Baltic coast is mainly fine and dry.

In the early autumn, Poland is usually sunny and there is hardly any rain, making this a particularly attractive time of year, especially in the mountains. Winter is not especially harsh in most parts of the country, with temperatures seldom dropping below -10°C (14°F), except in the north-east, where it is colder. In the eastern part of Poland and in the mountains there are heavy snowfalls, providing ample opportunity for winter sports. With its scenery and climate, therefore, this country between the Baltic and the Carpathians has something to offer holidaymakers all the year round.

Economy

Five years after the end of socialism and the change to a free-market economy, the statistics revealed improvements in the Polish economy although these were not, and are unlikely to be for some time, reflected in the living standards of the population. Poland's geographical position allows the easy importation of raw materials and access to markets in the East and West. It is the largest market in Central Europe with 25 percent of the population under the age of 15 and a well-educated adult workforce. In 1993, with a rise in the Gross National Product of 3 percent, Poland was the first country in the former Eastern bloc to achieve a positive balance of trade figures (with the exception of the former German Democratic Republic). Nevertheless, the economy is still struggling due to factors that are often attributed to 40 years of financial mismanagement by the socialists.

Factory fumes

Over 25 percent of the workforce is in agriculture, growing wheat, barley, sugar beet, potatoes and fodder crops. Farming has always been done on a small scale and has largely been in private hands. Now small and medium-sized business enterprises and some of the giant state concerns have been privatised. But much of the euphoria of the initial post-Communist years has evaporated: with high unemployment, the impoverishment of large sectors of society and spectacular crashes of particular firms, the population has discovered through bitter experience that mismanagement can occur even under capitalism.

Harvest time

In 1989 the democratic governments inherited a rocketing inflation rate, which had reached three figures and could only be halted in January 1990 by means of horrendous price rises and the introduction of monetarist economic reform by the then deputy prime minister Jacek Balcerowicz. Since then, inflation has remained a problem and is still much too high for a stable economy to be achieved in the medium term. In addition, foreign debt is also a burden. There are thus still many obstacles to be overcome if the country's economic development is to be sustainable.

Displaying Solidarity

Government

The Republic of Poland is a parliamentary democracy of the classic Western type. In the parliament, which consists of two houses: the Sejm, the lower house with 460 members, is the highest legislative organ and controls the government; the Senate, the upper house of parliament with 100 members, participates in the legislative process. The government is the highest body in the land, the next administrative level consists of the 49 political departments into which the country is divided.

At the top of the hierarchy is the president, who is the head of state.The first president is the former worker's leader Lech Walesa. The government is led by the prime minister, who commands a majority in the Sejm and who elects a council of ministers.

Lech Walesa's house

Establishing a parliamentary democracy after the collapse of communism was no easy task; the disunity between the numerous parties and interest groups frequently resulted in government crises, political instability or stagnation. The system has now largely stabilised and the introduction of electoral reforms gives a certain continuity in the country's political development.

Nature and the environment

Almost a third of Poland is covered by forest, primarily pine, spruce and mixed deciduous and coniferous forest. Botanists have identified thousands of types of plants in Poland, including over 1,200 lichens and almost 1,500 of the more complex species of fungus. In the spring, the fields and meadows are a sea of flowers.

The Polish forests are home to numerous species of animal that have become extinct in other European countries, such as the brown bear, elk and wolf. In Masuria, visitors are immediately struck by the large numbers of storks who build their huge nests on almost every gable and church tower; in spring the villages are filled with the sound of their clappering.

Poland is a paradise for bird-watchers in every respect. The Bierbrzanski National Park in the northeast is a huge marshy area which, in spite, or perhaps precisely because of its inaccessibility, attracts ornithologists from all over the world. In the Wolinski National Park on the Baltic coast, on the general tourist route, amateurs can spot one of the very rare European sea eagles which are the model for the Polish national emblem.

Strategic look-out

The Bialowieska National Park is the oldest forest park in the country. It is a protected area covering 50sq km (19 sq miles) of the vast impenetrable forest that extends on either side of the Belorussian border and it is home to the last European bison. Virtually extinct after World War I, they were reintroduced into this area and now number almost 300. The rare tarpan, a wild pony, and wild boar are also to be found in this park, which is on UNESCO's World Natural Heritage list and can only be visited with a park ranger.

Bison

Although Poland is still a popular destination for nature lovers, in many parts of the country the ravages of environmental pollution are all too plain to see. Poland's worst problems are caused by the use of coal and brown coal, the country's main source of energy, the devastating consequences of which are most evident in the industrial zone of Upper Silesia, the industrial heart of Poland.

The damage is far-reaching: the acid rain is not only attacking trees and buildings but human health suffered too; the rate of respiratory illness, cancer and deformities in newborn babies is significantly higher than anywhere else. In Upper Silesia, where almost half the waste gases in Poland are emitted, life expectancy (66 for men and 75 for women) is lower for men than the national average.

The country's water has also been effected by the over-exploitation of natural resources, and today the Vistula is one of the most heavily polluted rivers in Europe.

While in the socialist era environmental problems were swept under the carpet, they have now become an important public issue. The government has responded by launching an investigation into levels of pollution, even though the ministry for environmental affairs expects strong resistance from the industrial sector at attempts to regulate industrial waste disposal.

A local of Zakopane

Population

Today Poland has a population of 38.5 million, almost all of whom are Poles. While at first this might seem a perfectly normal state of affairs, in the thousand-year history of the country it is rather the exception. For centuries

Poland was a multinational state, the home not only to Poles but also Russians, Belorussians, Ukrainians, Slovakians, Latvians, Lithuanians and Jews as well as large numbers of Germans, in particular Prussians and Silesians.

Symbol of statehood

A uniform Polish national state was only created after World War II. This was a painful process, not only for the many Germans, who were driven out of their homeland, but also for the Polish inhabitants of large areas of former East Poland, who suffered the same fate at the hands of Stalin. At his instigation, Polish territory was shifted a considerable distance to the west, and whether from Wilno or Lwow, Warsaw or Poznan, after World War II every third Pole was either living in exile or homeless. Now that the Polish borders have been recognised by all parties, relationships between the Poles and the few members of national minorities such as the Ukrainians, Belorussians and in particular the Germans, who populate the villages around Opole, have noticeably improved in recent years.

Religion

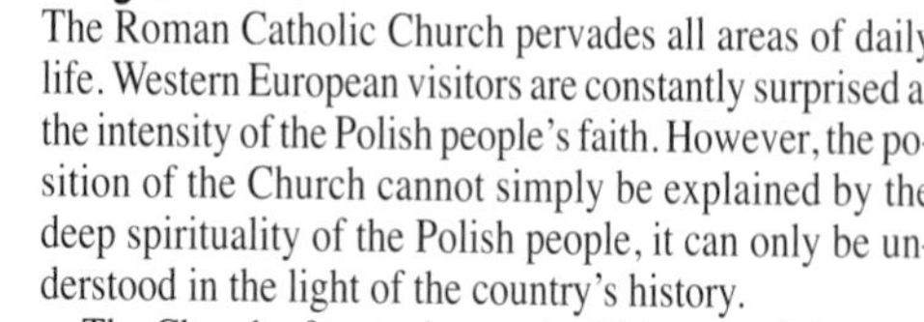

The Roman Catholic Church pervades all areas of daily life. Western European visitors are constantly surprised at the intensity of the Polish people's faith. However, the position of the Church cannot simply be explained by the deep spirituality of the Polish people, it can only be understood in the light of the country's history.

Wayside shrine

The Church often took upon itself the role of the state during periods of foreign occupation and provided spiritual strength in times of national crises. This patriarchal position inevitably brought the Church into violent conflict with the atheistic, socialist government after World War II.

This conflict was one of the factors that contributed to the decline of the Communist system. There has always been a bond between the Church and the people and it supported them in the darkest periods of this century. Throughout the occupation by Nazi Germany and the terrors of the Stalinist regime, as well as the persistent endeavours of the Communist leaders to change Poland, the Church held firm. In 1976, when the Polish conference of bishops published a pastoral in which the Roman Catholic Church was portrayed as the legitimate representative of the people and the nation, it received the people's unanimous approval. The election of Cardinal Karol Wojtyla as Pope in 1978 strengthened this claim still further. A year later, on his first journey home, the Pope encouraged millions of his countrymen with the words: 'Do not be afraid!'

War memorial

But today the Church no longer has an opponent which it can confront in cooperation with the people, its social significance has changed. Now, many practising, believing Catholics are more likely to react with irritation to the constant interference of the Church in politics. Nevertheless, all this has had little effect on the traditional piety which has always been an expression of the country's cultural, national and social life. The Catholic Church has even established its own national radio station, Radio Maria, based in Torun and funded by private donations.

Oliwa Cathedral: detail

Traditions and customs

Although they have a strong religious content, many of the Easter customs are of pagan origin. The entire country gets into the holiday mood several days before Easter, with colourful market stalls selling painted Easter eggs, sugar lambs and bundles of evergreen and catkins.

On Palm Sunday palm leaves are dedicated following the Christian tradition; the celebration of Christ's entry into Jerusalem is the highlight of the day in many towns, with the most famous Palm Sunday procession taking place in Kalwaria Zebrzydowska near Cracow. The most unusual and colourful of the Easter customs are the parades and dances of the Guards of the Tomb of Christ.

On Easter Monday a sudden chilly awakening is in store for women. The custom of *Smigus Dyngus* ranges from a discreet spraying with perfume of those selected for the honour to the coarse village version where a bucket of water is tipped over them instead. The origin of this tradition is quite unknown.

The celebrations on Midsummer's Eve, on 21 June, are more folklore-orientated: at night rivers and lakes are transformed by garlands of flowers with burning candles (*wianki*), that are set afloat on the water. There is a general holiday atmosphere with public festivals, dances, boat parades and fireworks.

The youth of today

Historical Highlights

120,000 years ago The oldest traces of mankind have been found in a cave in the valley of the Pradnik River in the area of the Cracow-Tschenstochau Plateau (Wyzyna Krakowsko-Czestochowska) northeast of Cracow.

Iron Age Archaeologists in the 1930s discovered an original Slavic settlement by Biskupin Lake, north of Gniezno, and in the well-preserved, wooden buildings, which date back 2,500 years, found artefacts from the Lusatian culture in the Iron Age.

375 The invasion of the Huns triggers the great migration of nations, during the course of which Slav tribes settle in the territory that is present-day Poland.

966 Considered to be the year that marks the founding of Poland. Mieszko I, a powerful Polian chief living in the Poznan region, is baptised. With his conversion to Christianity he places himself under the protection of Rome and extends the boundaries of his state to include Silesia and Malopolska (Little Poland).

992 Boleslaw I Chrobry (the Brave), the son of Mieszko, whose domain for a time even included Lusatia, Bohemia and Kiev, is crowned first king of Poland.

1000 In Gniezno the first Polish church province is established. The German Emperor Otto III visits the city and is accorded a friendly welcome.

1138 After the death of Boleslaw III Krzywousty (Boleslaus the Wry-mouthed), the kingdom is divided according to his formula for succession between his four sons; whoever rules Cracow is senior to the others and hence politically more powerful. This results in prolonged internal conflicts as a result of which Poland loses its international importance.

1226 Duke Konrad Mazowiecki summons the German Order of Knighthood to Poland to support him in his struggle against the Prussians.

1241 A Polish army under Henryk Pobozny stops the Mongol advance at Legnica. Cracow is burnt down.

1309 The Order of Knighthood has consolidated its power and rules over a large territory along the Eastern Baltic Sea, including the Hanseatic city of Gdansk.

1320 Wladyslaw Lokietek, Prince of Sieradz, succeeds in reuniting a large part of Polish territory and is crowned king.

1325 Polish-Lithuanian alliance is formed against the Teutonic Knights.

1333 Kazimierz III inherits the crown from his father. He is one of Poland's most important rulers, known as Kazimierz III Wielki (Casimir the Great). He doubles the size of his realm and, by expanding to the east, transforms Poland into a multinational state.

1364 Founding of Cracow University.

1386 Lithuania and Poland are united through the marriage of Jagiello, Grand Duke of Lithuania, with the Polish queen Jadwiga (d'Anjou). Under the Jagiellon dynasty, the country flourishes both culturally and economically.

1410 The victory over the Teutonic Knights at the Battle of Grunwald/Tannenberg establishes the preconditions for a greater expansion of power in the unified realm.

1466 In the Second Peace of Torun, The German Order of Knighthood recognises the sovereignty of the Polish kings and cedes territory at the mouth of the River Vistula, including the city of Gdansk, to Poland. The Jagiellons now rule from the Black Sea to the Baltic.

1505 At the Imperial Diet of Radom the king grants unprecedented and extensive rights to the nobility. Thereby 'rule of the nobility' is established as a specific Polish form of government.

1543 Nicholas Copernicus publishes *De revolutionibus orbium Coelestium*, his book on planetary motion.

1552 A decision of the Imperial Diet establishes the right of religious freedom. The cultural and denominational tolerance thus afforded makes

Poland a haven of tranquillity in the turmoil of the religious wars engulfing Europe.

1564 The Jesuits are called into the country, heralding the start of the counter-reformation.

1569 With the Union of Lublin, Poland and Lithuania are formally united into a single state. Warsaw becomes the seat of the joint parliament, the Sejm.

1573–1791 The period of 'elected kings', when the royal succession is based not on inheritance but election by the aristocracy.

1618–48 Thirty Years' War in Central Europe.

1621 East Prussia falls to the Elector of Brandenburg. The fate of this region is henceforth determined in Berlin.

1655–60 War with Sweden.

1772, 1793, 1795 Partly as a consequence of the anachronistic political system and the anarchy resulting from an aristocracy with far too much power the country – already divided into three parts – is an easy prey for its neighbours Prussia, Austria and Russia. The reforms that are introduced come too late.

1830–1, 1863–4 The two most important uprisings (the November Insurrection and the January Insurrection) against Czarist Russia are brutally crushed.

1892 Foundation of the Polish Socialist Party.

1918 After the end of World War I, the defeat of the Central Powers and the revolution in Russia, Poland is reborn. Marshall Józef Pilsudski is in charge of the new state, even though he has no official function for much of the interwar period. Redefining the borders of the resurrected state is a problem and the eastern boundary is established through armed conflict.

1920 Poland stops the advance of the Red Army at the Vistula and occupies part of the Ukraine and Lithuania. Gdansk becomes a 'free city'.

1921 After heavy fighting between Poles and Germans, Upper Silesia is divided at a conference of ambassadors.

1939 On 1 September, German troops invade Poland, an action which triggers World War II; on 17 September the Red Army marches into eastern Poland. The German army quickly defeats the poorly equipped Polish army and the Nazis subsequently occupy the country; by the end of the war almost 6 million Polish citizens have lost their lives.

1945 After the end of World War II the new borders of Poland are established by the victorious powers at Yalta and Potsdam; at Stalin's request, Polish territory is moved from east to west. Soon afterwards the Communists – officially the Polish United Workers' Party, PZPR – take power.

1955 Founding of the 'Warsaw Pact' with the Soviet Union and other Eastern bloc states.

1981 After 18 months of political conflict and strikes, spearheaded by the independent trade union Solidarity (Solidarnosc) – founded under the leadership of the Gdansk shipyard worker, Lech Walesa – General Wojciech Jaruzelski, the head of the Party and government and under pressure from the Soviet Union, proclaims martial law on 13 December. Solidarity is prohibited, thousands of activists are arrested.

1989 As a result of the changes taking place within the Soviet Union and the economic chaos in Poland, the Communist leadership starts official negotiations with the opposition and in June partially free elections are held. Tadeusz Mazowiecki becomes prime minister. The country embarks on the difficult task of establishing a parliamentary democracy and market economy.

1990 Germany formally recognises the western border of Poland at the Oder/Neisse line. Lech Walesa wins the presidential election in November.

1993 The remains of exiled war-time leader General Sikorski are flown home. Poland's first woman prime minister, Hanna Suchocka, resigns. The last of the 60,000 Polish troops based in Poland leave.

1994 Poland applies for membership of the European Union.

1995 50th anniversary of the liberation of Auschwitz.

Medals from another epoch

Preceding pages: Bieszczcady panorama

Route 1

★★★ Warsaw – the phoenix risen from the ashes *See map on page 18*

Krasinski Palace

Warsaw (pop. 1.7 million) is a lively metropolis, the cultural centre of Poland, an amalgam of past, present and future, where lovingly preserved historical buildings, pompous reminders of Stalinism and the marble office palaces of international firms stand side by side. The inhabitants themselves do not appear to be particularly impressed by the historic ground beneath their hurrying feet, as they go about their everyday business in the capital. The feeling of a new departure after the fall of Communism has largely evaporated, and only a few people have succeeded in realising their dreams of a better standard of living or even wealth. Many Poles were plunged into a new poverty by the new system.

History

The Madonna looms large

In the course of its 700-year history, the city has had more than its share of catastrophes, the greatest of which was World War II. The devastation of the wars with Sweden, the occupation by Russia and the insurrections during the partition of Poland did not leave their mark on the people of Warsaw to anything like the same extent as the horrors of the last war, which brought years of terror and the obliteration of a large section of the population. Many people were deported to Germany and subjected to forced labour or were sent to concentration camps.

The darkest aspect of the German occupation was undoubtedly that of the Warsaw Ghetto. From 1940, all the Jewish inhabitants of the city were crammed into an increasingly diminishing area. Goods trains left daily for the extermination camp Treblinka 100 km (60 miles) away. As the situation for the few people remaining in the ghetto became increasingly hopeless, they resolved to make a final stand: the uprising of the Warsaw Ghetto took place in April 1943. In the unequal battle, the SS units had no difficulty crushing the rebellion, and razed the whole ghetto area to the ground.

The Warsaw Uprising of 1 August 1944, initiated by the exiled government in London, was equally unsuccessful: in 63 days of fierce fighting 200,000 people, most of them civilians, lost their lives either as a result of mass executions or bombings. The Red Army, although already on the outskirts of Warsaw, did not intervene. When it did eventually march in, 80 percent of the city had been systematically destroyed and it was almost deserted.

Rebuilding began immediately after the end of the war. Visitors to modern-day Warsaw cannot begin to imagine the extent of the devastation.

Sights

A tour of Warsaw can take a day or several days depending on how much time you have. The walk through the Old Town is designed to take up one day. In order to visit the National Museum and the Castle another day is required, and at least one more day is necessary for the excursion to Wilanow. For Wilanow and the site of the former ghetto, the Palace of Culture and Science and the Lazienki Palace, you will need to take public transport or use your car. The New Town, the Royal Way (Trakt Królewski) and the Old Town should only be explored on foot.

The Palace of Culture and Science

Wherever you are in the city, the massive ★ **Palace of Culture and Science** ❶ is impossible to miss. Right in the centre of Warsaw, the building, put up in 1952–5, is a perfect example of 'wedding-cake' architecture. A present from the Soviet Union to its Polish 'brothers', it was intended to demonstrate the superiority of Stalinism: with 3,288 rooms on 30 floors, it towers 235m (771ft) into the sky, disappearing into the haze that frequently hangs over the city. Today, the capital's Stalinist heirloom is a burden with its immense maintenance costs. Many rooms have acquired new functions and branches of affluent Western companies, gaming halls and offices have established themselves there alongside cultural institutes.

Walk north past All Souls Church to the **Synagogue** ❷. This rather inconspicuous building, which was restored with the help of American Jews, is hidden behind modern houses and is now the meeting place of the few remaining Warsaw Jews. A few minutes' walk to the east is the **Protestant Church** ❸ (zbor ewangelicko-augsburski). The neoclassical rotunda, a circular building with

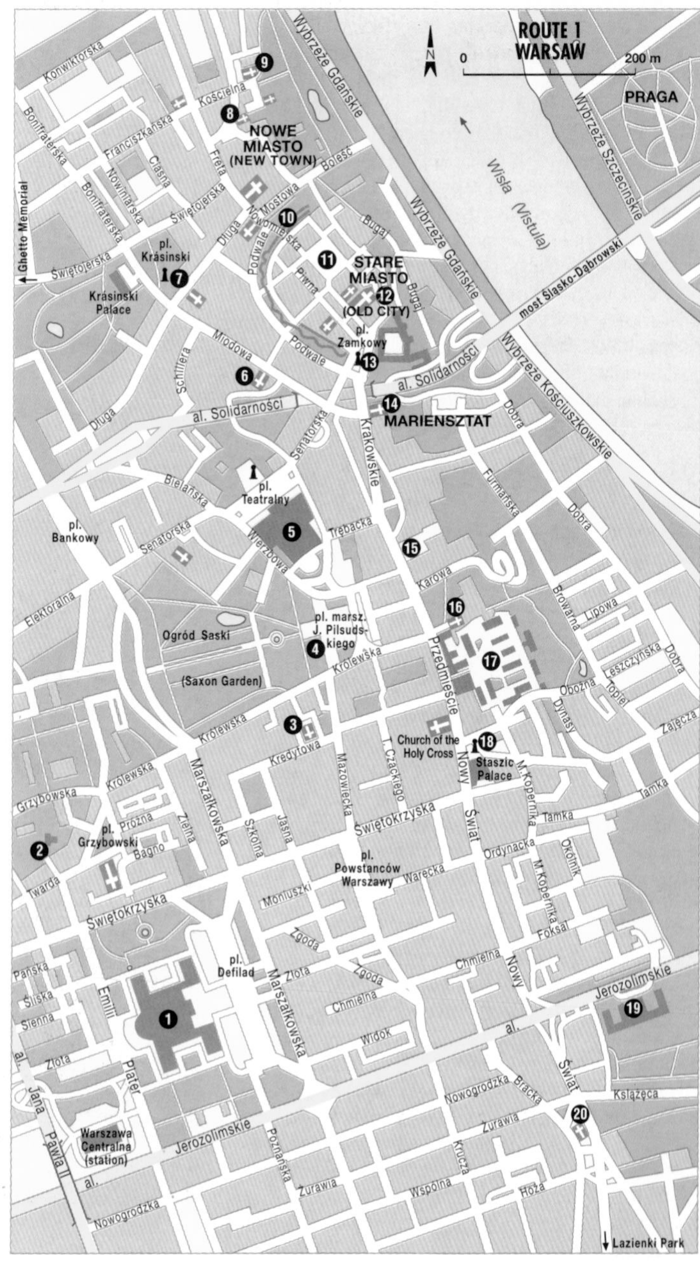
ROUTE 1
WARSAW
0
200 m
N
PRAGA
NOWE
MIASTO
(NEW TOWN)
STARE
MIASTO
(OLD CITY)
MARIENSZTAT
Wisła (Vistula)
Ghetto Memorial
pl. Krásinski
Krásinski Palace
pl. Zamkowy
pl. Teatralny
pl. Bankowy
Ogród Saski
(Saxon Garden)
pl. marsz. J. Pilsudskiego
Church of the Holy Cross
Staszic Palace
pl. Grzybowski
pl. Powstanców Warszawy
pl. Defilad
Warszawa Centralna (station)
Lazienki Park
Konwiktorska
Bonifraterska
Kościelna
Franciszkańska
Nowiniarska
Ciasna
Freta
Świętojerska
Długa
Mostowa
Nowomiejska
Podwale
Piwna
Bugaj
Boleść
Wybrzeże Gdańskie
Wybrzeże Szczecińskie
most Śląsko-Dąbrowski
Wybrzeże Kościuszkowskie
al. Solidarności
Miodowa
Schillera
Senatorska
Krakowskie
Bielańska
Dobra
Furmańska
Trębacka
Wierzbowa
Karowa
Elektoralna
Królewska
Przedmieście
Browarna
Lipowa
Leszczyńska
Oboźna
Topiel
Dynasy
Zajęcza
Kredytowa
Mazowiecka
T. Czackiego
Nowy Świat
M. Kopernika
Tamka
Grzybowska
Próżna
Zielna
Marszałkowska
Szkolna
Jasna
Świętokrzyska
Ordynacka
Okólnik
Bagno
Twarda
Warecka
Moniuszki
Foksal
Zgoda
Chmielna
Pańska
Śliska
Sienna
Emilii
Plater
Złota
Widok
al. Jerozolimskie
Jana Pawła II
Nowogrodzka
Bracka
Książęca
Żurawia
Poznańska
Krucza
Wspólna
Hoża
1
2
3
4
5
6
7
8
9
10
11
12
13
14
15
16
17
18
19
20

a lantern dome dating from 1781, was rebuilt after the war, by contrast with the former Saxon Palace nearby, where all that remains is a fragment of the arcade. This is now the location of the **Tomb of the Unknown Soldier** ❹ (Grob Neiznanego Zolnierza): at the end of World War I soil was collected in urns from the battlefields from all over the world where Polish soldiers had fallen. The **changing of the guard** takes place here at noon every day and is one of Warsaw's tourist attractions. Behind the tomb are the **Saxon Gardens** (Ogrod Saski), the ideal place for both the local people and footsore tourists to rest for a while from the hustle and bustle of city life and the Warsaw traffic.

Tomb of the Unknown Soldier

Walk through the park to the imposing building known as the **Grand Theatre** ❺ (Teatr Wielki). This building, with its facade by the Italian architect Antonio Corazzi, is a superb example of neoclassical architecture. With almost 2,000 seats, it is the largest opera house in Poland. On the opposite side of Theatre Square the **Monument to the Heroes of Warsaw** commemorates the fighters and victims of the German occupation of the city from 1939–45. It depicts Nike, the goddess of victory, who, with raised sword, is storming against imaginary attackers.

Monument to the Warsaw Uprising

The route continues on ulica Senatorska and ulica Miodowa past magnificent city palaces to the baroque **Capuchin Church** ❻, dating from the 17th century – in the wall of one of the chapels is the heart of its founder, King Jan III Sobieski – past the **Monument to the Warsaw Uprising** ❼, the design of which has been a source of considerable controversy, to the baroque ★ **Krasinski Palace**. This palace with its elegant facade was designed by the Dutch architect Tylman van Gameren in 1677. The building is decorated with two tympana by the young Andreas Schlüter, from the period before he was engaged by the Berlin court and began his rapid rise to fame. Today the Krasinski Palace houses the **National Library**, which includes a valuable collection of manuscripts. The palace and the surrounding park are on the western edge of the New Town, which, contrary to its name, is a historic district of the city near the Old Town and is the high point of the city tour.

Heroes of the Ghetto

Those doing the tour by car can make a detour from here to the ★ **Monument to the Heroes of the Ghetto Uprising** in ulica Zamenhofa. It was here that Willy Brandt knelt in 1970 in remembrance of the victims of the Nazi atrocities. Car drivers should look for a parking place near Krasinski Square, if not before, since the crooked streets of the old ★ **New Town** are best explored on foot, and the whole area of the Old Town is in any case a pedestrian precinct.

Rising above the New Town Square (Rynek Nowego Miasta) is the dome of the **Church of the Nuns of the Holy Sacrament** ❽, a fine building with a monastery, also the work of Tylman van Gameren, the foremost architect in the Polish baroque era. Looking in the direction of the Vistula river (Wisla), you will see the bell tower of the **Gothic Church of the Visitation of the Virgin Mary** ❾. From the terrace on the east side of the church there is a view across the Vistula to the suburb of Praga opposite.

Facade detail, Old Town Square

The Old Town

The ★★ **Old Town** was first created in the 13th century but it was reduced to a heap of rubble during World War II. Since then it has been completely rebuilt in its original form, using designs from the highly detailed city views by the 18th-century, Italian artist Bernardo Belotto, or his uncle Canaletto. In its present form, the oldest district of Warsaw is thus a 20th-century creation – a masterpiece of Polish restoration work, which has earned the UNESCO designation of a site of World Cultural Heritage.

The Barbican

The Barbican ❿, a massive structure dating from the 16th century, marks the entry into the Old Town. Inside the Barbican, and also in front of it in fine weather, a wide range of modern art is offered for sale. The market place and focal point of the Old Town is the **Old Town Square** ⓫ (Rynek Starego Miasta), which is surrounded by handsome burghers' houses, orginally dating from the 15th to 19th centuries. It is a favourite gathering place for both residents and tourists, who meet to tour the pubs of the Old Town or sit outside at one of the many café tables in fine weather. Young artists converge on the square to sell portraits and a wide range of views of the Old Town. Horse-drawn carriages can also be hired here by those who have had enough of walking.

The Old Town Square

From the square, it is only a few minutes' walk past the Jesuit Church, to **St John's Cathedral** ⓬, the largest church in the Old Town. Many rulers and important people are buried here, including the great Polish writer Henryk Sienkiewicz (*Quo Vadis?*). The Gothic building with its impressive star-vaulting dates back to the 14th century.

On the south side of the Old Town is the ★ **Royal Castle** ⓭, where the magnificent interiors have been reconstructed in minute detail. Some of the original furnishings were stored elsewhere during the war to save them from destruction. It was not until 1971 that rebuilding of the palace was begun, a task that took almost 20 years to complete. In front of the castle is the Castle Square with the **Column of Sigismund III Vasa**, a popular photo-stop for visitors

Column of Sigismund III

to Warsaw. The figure on the column with its huge cross is often taken for a church leader; but it was the Counter-Reformatory zeal of this particular king that inspired the sculptor to put a cross in his hands.

Radziwill Palace and guard

After leaving the Old Town you will find yourself on the ★ **Royal Way** (Trakt Krolewski), an elegant boulevard connecting the Royal Castle with **Wilanow Palace**. It is lined with prestigious buildings, and some sections are very busy. **St Anne's Church** ⓮ is the first building of interest at the beginning of the Royal Way. Originally Gothic, dating from the second half of the 15th century, it was rebuilt a number of times and the present building is in the neoclassical style. The facade is clearly modelled on a church in Venice, Il Redentore, built by the 16th-century Italian architect Andrea Palladio.

Further down, the road widens into an elongated square with lawns and flowerbeds in the middle. Here, a statue of the great Polish national romantic poet Adam Mickiewicz (1789–1855) appears to be looking down condescendingly from his pedestal at the hustle and bustle below.

Of the many palaces along the Royal Way, only the **Radziwill Palace** ⓯ will be mentioned here. Once owned by the Radziwill family, it is without doubt one of the most impressive buildings on the avenue. It is also known as the Viceroy's Palace, as in 1819 it was used as the residence of the Viceroy of the Kingdom of Poland. It has been an official state building ever since, witnessing countless official receptions and the signing of important national documents. In the inner courtyard is a statue of Napoleonic war hero, the Prince and Marshall of France Jozef Poniatowski, sculpted by the famous Danish artist Bertel Thorvaldsen in 1832. The original was destroyed during the war and the one that can be seen today was recreated from the replica kept in Copenhagen.

Jozef Poniatowski

Between the residences of the great families of Poland is the late baroque **Church of the Nuns of the Visitation** ⓰ which has an elaborate facade embellished with columns and a decorative rococo interior. Many consider it the most beautiful baroque church in Warsaw, but visitors must make up their own minds on this point.

Victim of reforms outside the Church of the Holy Cross

The boulevard continues to the **university** ⓱. The palaces which once belonged to the Tyszkiewicz and Uruski families and the former Kazimierzowski Royal Palace are now used as centres of research and teaching. Few universities are housed in such beautiful buildings.

Chopin enthusiasts will want to visit the **Church of the Holy Cross** diagonally opposite the university grounds: in the left-hand pillar of the main nave is an urn containing the heart of Frederic Chopin.

Another great man, Poland's famous 16th-century astronomer Nicholas Copernicus (*see Route 5, page 47*), is commemorated on the opposite side of the road. The **Copernicus Monument** ⓲, also by Thorvaldsen (1830), is situated in front of the Staszic Palace, a neoclassical building dating from the 19th century which now houses the Polish Academy of Sciences. At this point a coffee break is in order, and the Nowy Swiat Café (on the corner of Nowy Swiat and Swietokrzyska) is just the place. International newspapers are provided here and entice the visitor to relax and enjoy the old-fashioned plush surroundings at leisure.

Copernicus

The Royal Way, this section of which is called Nowy Swiat (New World), continues into the centre of modern Warsaw, where the first stop is the ★ **National Museum** ⓳. Early Christian frescoes from Pharos in Sudan, rescued by Polish archaeologists from the waters of the Aswan Dam, medieval sculptures and examples of Polish art from the last 200 years are the highlights of the museum's collections.

A little further south, the tour ends at **St Alexander's Church** ⓴. This neoclassical building, erected in 1818, stands with traffic surging round it all day on an island in the middle of the road, with the attractive name of Square of the Three Crosses (plac Trzech Krzyzy).

By this time, if not before, even good walkers will be thankful for a bus ride.

Lazienki Park

Lazienki Park

The bus route (nos. 116, 122, 193) to ★★ **Lazienki Park** follows the Aleje Ujazdowskie, which is a grand avenue lined with buildings each combining a variety of styles, many of which house embassies, and where the office of the prime minister is located. The park, which was first opened to the public as long ago as 1818, is a haven of peace in the middle of a roaring metropolis. At the centre is **Lazienki Palace**, the summer residence of the last king of Poland, Stanislaw August II Poniatowski, until his abdication in 1795. No one would guess that this magnificent building started life as a bath house.

The neighbouring **Theatre on the Island**, dating from 1790, was modelled on an ancient theatre ruin. The canal separating the stage from the audience stand made it possible to include boats in the productions. The park has a number of fine neoclassical and romantic buildings, including the Myslewicki Palace, the Temple of Diana, the White House (Bialy Domek) and the President's residence, Belvedere Palace, monuments to the craftsmanship of the architects and landscape gardeners responsible for Lazienki. In the upper part of the park, near the Aleje Ujazdowskie, under a weeping willow is a statue of Poland's most famous composer Frederic Chopin (*see page 78*) in meditative pose. In the summer, every Sunday at noon an audience of all ages gathers by this Art Nouveau monument to listen to a live concert of Chopin's mazurkas and polonaises.

Lazienki Palace and lake

Chopin concerts every Sunday

Wilanow

Take a bus (No 180), tram or taxi to reach ★★ **Wilanow Park and Palace** (Wednesday to Monday 10am–4pm) on the city boundary. The former summer residence of King Jan III Sobieski, who defeated the Turks in the Battle of Vienna in 1683, is located on the southern edge of Warsaw. Wilanow Palace is considered by many to be the most beautiful secular baroque building in Poland. Set in a huge park, it still has all the grandeur of a royal residence. The rooms of the palace were restored after the war and furnished with the original inventory. In addition to the historic furniture and valuable pottery, the famous collection of portraits by Polish artists from the 16th to the 19th century is particularly worth seeing: look out for the large painting of the early 19th-century owner of the palace, antique collector and archaeologist Stanislaw Kostka Potocki, by Jacques-Louis David.

Wilanow Palace detail

Whether as a mass of blossom in the spring or a shady retreat in the summer, whether golden in the autumn or snow-covered in winter, the Palace Park is enchanting in every season. The gardens, laid out in the English style, extend to the former tributary of the Vistula. Dotted among the old trees are a Japanese bridge, an artificial lake and a Chinese pagoda.

In the enchanting park

The international reputation of the Polish poster school makes a visit to the **Poster Museum** (Tuesday to Sunday 10am–4pm) in the former riding school almost obligatory. The posters are a vivid record of Poland's postwar history.

Route 2

The Baltic coast

★★ Szczecin – Swinoujscie – Kolobrzeg – ★ Slupsk – ★★★ Gdansk (652km/408 miles)

If what you want to do is to relax on a beach, this route, which follows the Baltic coast, is just for you. It is also ideal for families with children. Gdansk, at the end of the route, not only provides a change after the seaside, it is also a must for all those interested in art or history. Rebuilt after the war, Gdansk is a masterpiece of Polish restoration work and is an essential part of any visit to Poland.

Tug boat in Szczecin

The starting point of this trip, Szczecin, has also retained something of its original appearance. The route leads through once fashionable resorts such as Kolberg and the scenically beautiful national parks of Wolinski and Slowinski are refuges for rare species of animal and plants which thrive in these protected environments.

Seven days are necessary in order to see all the sights and also have time to relax on the beaches of the Baltic.

ROUTES 2, 4 & 5

0 50 km

BALTIC SEA

Słowiński P.N. · Łeba · Kluki · Jez. Gardno · Jez. Łebsko · Mierzeja Helska · Hel · Ustka · Wejherowo · Darłowo · Słupsk · Lębork · Rumia · Gdynia · Sopot · Gdansk · Kartuzy · Słupia · Kołobrzeg · Koszalin · Bytów · Wolinski P.N. · Tczew · Świnoujście · Kamień Pomorski · Kościerzyna · Zalew Szczecinski · Miastko · Starogard G. · Malbork · Świdwin · Gniew · Wisła · Szczecinek · Chojnice · Police · Kwidzyn · Szczecin · Drawsko Pomorskie · Grudziądz · Berlin · Stargard Szcz. · Świecie · Złotów · Wałcz · Chełmno · Choszczno · Piła · Bydgoszcz · Toruń · Noteć · Gorzów Wielkopolski · Ciechocinek · Odra · Oder · Drezdenko · Wągrowiec · Biskupin · Inowrocław · Warta · Radziejów · Frankfurt (Oder) · Włocławek · Międzyrzecz · Gniezno · Poznan · Września · GERMANY · Kórnik · Świebodzin · Rogalin · Konin · Koło · Śrem · Katowice

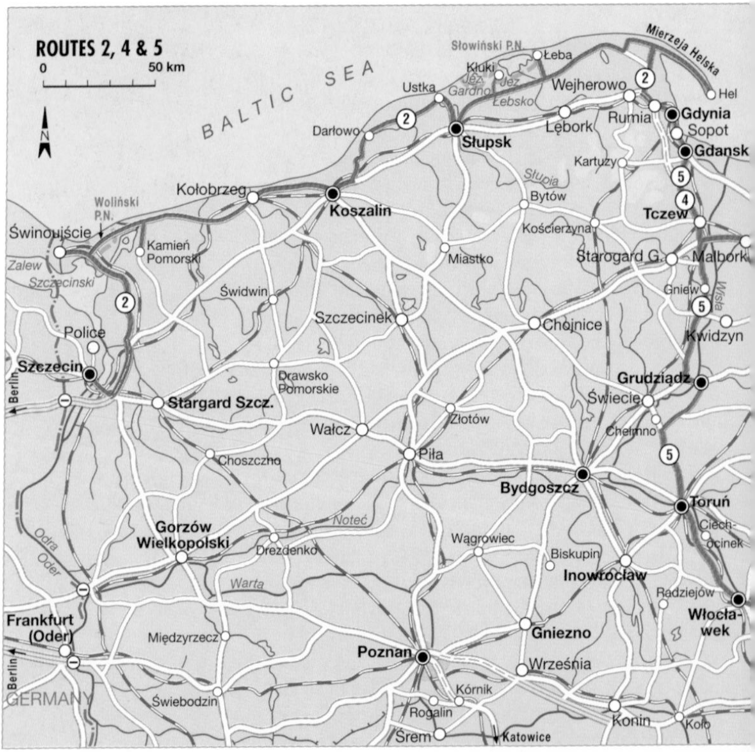

Since the coast is well provided with tourist facilities, it is not usually necessary to reserve rooms in advance during the holiday season. However, if you have a tent with you your choice of accommodation will be widened considerably, as there is a plentiful supply of camping and bivouac sites.

Church of St Peter and St Paul with Hanseatic symbol

The capital of West Pomerania in the northwest of Poland, ★★ **Szczecin** (pop. 410,000) is an old Hanseatic town very close to the German border and it makes no attempt to conceal the fact that until World War II it was German. However, the history of Szczecin, formerly Stettin, is not solely dominated by its German past, but by the fact that for centuries this harbour town used to be a bone of contention between Poland, Denmark and Brandenburg, between Prussians, French and Swedes – the tragic fate of a place with excellent strategic and economic properties that made it particularly desirable.

Many important buildings were lost in the battles between the various contenders, but the worst damage was done by the heavy bombing of World War II. The prestigious buildings of the terrace, ★ **Waly Chrobrego ❶**,

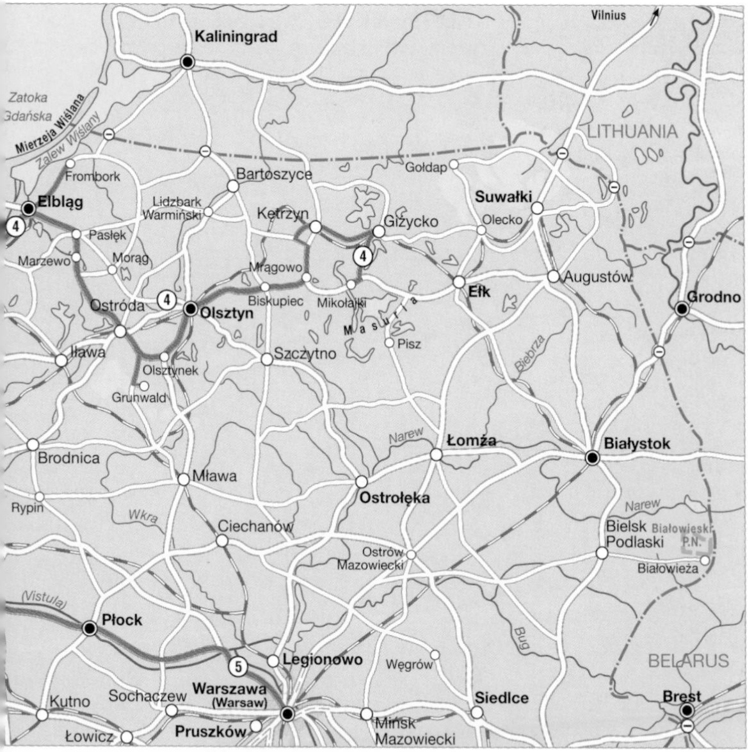

View from the Palace Tower

Old Town Hall, gable detail

which dominate the banks of the River Odra, are Szczecin's most striking feature. Built early in the 20th century, they include part of the National Museum with its archaeological, ethnographical and maritime collections.

From here it is only a short distance to the **Bastion of the Seven Coats** ❷, a fortified tower with 4-m (13-ft) thick walls which stood up to the bombs of the last war. Above the bastion, looking out over the Odra, is the impressive ★ **Palace of the Dukes of Pomerania** ❸. This residence originally housed the dukes' valuable collection of art treasures; these were later plundered by the Prussians who converted the rooms into a brewery. Although after 1945 the palace was renovated in the style of a typical 16th-century Renaissance residence, the building still has some of its original Gothic elements.

Only a few paces away from the palace and also on the banks of the Odra is the **Old Town Hall** ❹. After the building went up in flames in 1944, it was rebuilt not in the baroque form that it had acquired in the 17th century but in its original Gothic form with the decorative facade typical of north German Hanseatic towns (*see page 31, Gdansk*). It provides an appropriate setting for the **Historical Museum** of Szczecin.

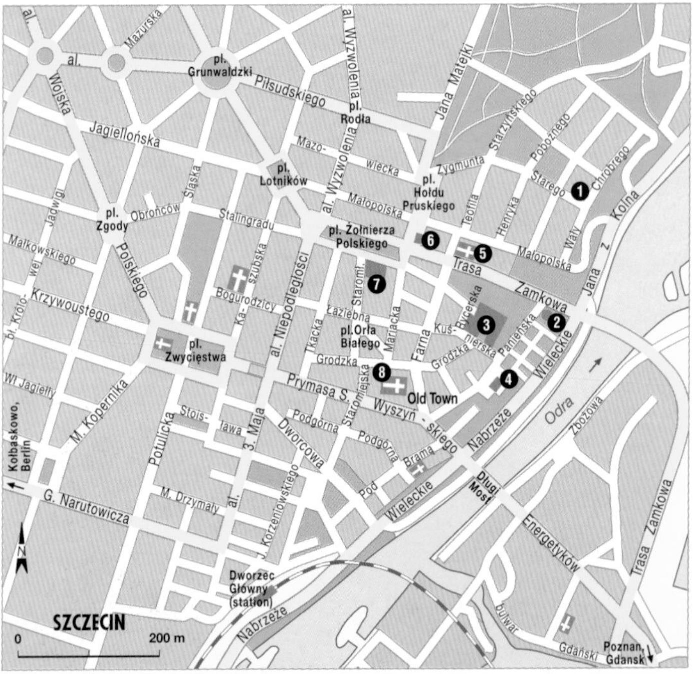

The Church of St Peter and St Paul ❺ is a good example of Pomeranian sacred architecture. The brick

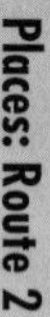

building, with its complex crow-step gable crowned by a rose window, has retained its Gothic appearance. The church exterior is decorated with glazed **terracotta heads** and the interior has a fine 18th-century wooden ceiling.

In Zwyciestwa Square is the magnificent **Gate of Prussian Homage** ❻ (brama Holdu Pruskiego), a reminder of the sale of the city by the Swedes to the Prussians in 1720. Just a few minutes' walk away from here are several restored 18th-century baroque palaces, one of which houses the **National Museum's** ❼ (Muzeum Narodowe) collection of medieval sculptures from Eastern Pomerania. In the neighbouring neoclassical **Palace of the Heads** (Palac pod Glowami) is a collection of works by contemporary Polish artists.

The largest building in Szczecin is ★ **St James's Cathedral** ❽, a few minutes' walk to the south. This was also no more than a burnt-out ruin after the war, and it was not until 1971 that work began on the restoration of what is one of the largest Gothic churches in Pomerania.

Stained glass in St James's

Terracotta head, Church of St Peter and St Paul

Swinoujscie (pop. 55,000), 100km (60 miles) away, is of a quite different character. Divided by the River Swina, the two parts connected only by ferry, the town is located on the islands of Uznam and Wolin. This estuary town is the ideal place for those in search of relaxation, with an established reputation as a bathing resort. The beach is one of the most beautiful on the Baltic coast and is certainly the most lively.

Wolin, one of the three islands which form the estuary delta of the Odra, is popular with animal lovers and above all ornithologists with its large variety of birds. In 1960 most of the island was turned into the ★ **Wolin National Park** (Wolinski Park Narodowy). This protected area, which covers 46sq km (18sq miles), has provided a stretch of ecologically intact territory for the last sea

Swinoujscie promenade

Wolin National park

Brooding Bison

Turquoise lake

Kolobrzeg: Town Hall detail

eagles living in the wild, and is also home to many other species of animals. Well-signposted paths enable the visitor to enjoy the scenic beauty of the old woods with their numerous turquoise-coloured lakes and the steep cliffs 100m (328ft) high on the Baltic coast. A visit to the **Natural History Museum** in Miedzyzdroje beforehand will enable you to get the most out of your trip round the park (Tuesday to Sunday 10am–5pm).

Opposite the island of Wolin on the right-hand bank of the River Dziwnow is **Kamien Pomorski** (pop. 10,000; 153km/96 miles), the old seat of the Kamien bishops. **St John's Cathedral**, originally Romanesque and rebuilt in the Gothic style in the 15th century, is a mecca for music lovers with its 17th-century baroque organ. The sound of this instrument in a building with astoundingly good acoustics is enjoyed by organists and audiences every year at the organ festival held in July and August.

The next stop is **Kolobrzeg** (pop. 44,000; 226km/140 miles). This town, at the mouth of the River Parseta, owes its existence to its salt springs. According to an old legend, a Pomeranian prince was once hunting in the woods when his faithful dog was attacked by a wild animal. When the hunter cleaned the wound at a nearby spring the dog whined in agony. After the water dried, its fur was white with salt crystals. Whether this story is true or not, it is known that Kolobrzeg was already famous in the 9th century for its salt deposits.

When the Prussian government put a stop to the salt mining in 1855 for economic reasons, the resourceful citizens of the town exploited the therapeutic value of their salt water springs instead. As a combination of spa and summer resort on the Baltic, Kolobrzeg grew to be Germany's foremost sea resort before the World War II, with half a million people staying overnight every year. The war left its mark here too, and few buildings of architectural interest have remained. The reconstructed ★ **St Mary's Cathedral**, a red brick building that dates back to the 14th century, dominates the town with its massive tower. To the right of the church is the neo-Gothic town hall, designed by Karl Friedrich Schinkel.

St Mary's Cathedral

From Kolobrzeg the route leads into the hinterland through the modern concrete-built town of **Koszalin** (pop. 120,000; 269km/167 miles). From here drivers can either take the quick route on the E28 to Slupsk or follow the coast via the picturesque village of ★ **Darlowo** with its Dukes' Castle and have a refreshing swim at Ustka.

★ **Slupsk** (pop. 100,000; 339km/211 miles) is the cultural centre of the region. On the bank of the River Slupia is the Renaissance **Dukes' Castle** dating from the 16th century. In the Middle Ages the harbour of Slupsk was used for the export of agricultural products, and the town was famous for its breweries and amber processing. The notorious **Witches' Tower** where, as its name suggests, witches were imprisoned and tortured, dates from the 15th century. The last witch trial was held in 1701, when a woman called Trina Papisten was convicted of witchery and burned at the stake. Slupsk has many other historic buildings, including the Dominican Church, St Mary's Church and the New Town Hall, and is a popular place for an excursion.

On the south bank of Lake Lebsko, surrounded by marshy meadows, woods and reedbeds, is **Kluki** (381km/237 miles), with its Kashubian half-timbered houses. The ★ **open-air museum** (*skansen*) gives a vivid picture of the lifestyle of the Slovincians who once settled this area. The Slovincians were skilled at adapting to the adversities of nature, as a visit to the museum reveals. One of their inventions consisted of strange-looking basket shoes to prevent their horses from sinking in the marsh.

Leba: dunes and the harbour

★ **Leba** (pop. 4,000; 443km/277 miles) is better known as a resort than as a fishing and harbour town. Although it received a town charter as long ago as 1357, it is more of a village outside the tourist season. The Leba of those days was in fact 2km (1¼ miles) east of where it is now; shifting dunes and floods threatened to engulf the settlement, so in 1570 the inhabitants moved on to firmer ground. The old fishermen's cottages have a lot of character, even if almost every second house is a souvenir shop or a fish and chip shop.

For nature lovers and hikers the high point of this trip is the nearby ★★ **Slowinski National Park** (Slowinski Park Narodowy). The main attraction of this biosphere reserve which covers an area of 18,000ha (44,478 acres) is its

The dunes are slowly shifting

Windsurfing off the Hel Peninsula

Fishing museum on the harbour

shifting dunes. They can be reached by rented bicycle or electric car, but if you want to climb up the huge hills of sand you must do so on foot. At a height of around 50m (164ft), the dunes are steadily moving, swallowing up even the forests in their path and, as a result, constitute one of the few desert areas in Europe. The park also includes two large lakes, Lake Lebsko and Lake Gardno. The latter is accessible to the public, but Lake Lebsko is a bird sanctuary, habitat of the rare great snipe.

Sand and beaches continue to feature along this route, and the next port of call is the famous **Hel Peninsula** (Mierzeja Helska). Around 200 years ago the present peninsula consisted of many small individual islands. In time the sand washed in by the tides joined them up to create the peninsula, which is only 200m (656ft) to 3km (1¾ miles) wide, but has a length of 35km (22 miles). It projects like a tongue into the Gulf of Gdansk and is a major tourist attraction. The peninsula is still freely accessible by road or rail. However, this unique natural phenomenon is at risk from the curiosity of visitors and the action of the tides so that access is likely to be limited in the near future. Dunes and pines are the dominant feature of the landscape, and the side facing the open sea with its sandy beach is ideal for bathing.

The 'capital' of the peninsula is ★ **Hel** (pop. 5,000; 558km/349 miles), situated at the far end of it. The road to the village leads through a prohibited military zone but visitors are waved through by amiable recruits. Right on the harbour is a **Fishing Museum** accommodated in a converted church. With its old fishermen's houses dating from the 18th century, the smell of tar and seaweed and the hustle and bustle of the harbour, this little fishing village is full of atmosphere. Hel is the home of the Kashubians, a Slavic people closely linked with Poland.

At this point, you may well feel tempted to go on a boat trip, if only on one of the ferries plying regularly between Hel and Gdansk. Car drivers will prefer, however, to complete the last stage of this route by land.

When the outline of the industrial town and port of **Gdynia** appears in the distance which, together with ★ **Sopot** and ★★★ **Gdansk** (652km/408 miles), form the 'Tri-city' with a total population of around 800,000, the sand in your shoes and the sharp pine needles on the car seats will be all that is left to remind you of the idyllic scenery of Hel that you have only just left behind. Do not however be deterred by the less inviting appearance of the big city. By the time you walk down St Mary's Street in the Main Town of Gdansk, if not long before, there will be no doubt in your mind that Gdansk is one of the most beautiful and interesting cities in Poland.

Artus Court, Gdansk

Route 3

★★★ Gdansk – bastion of Teutonic Knights to cradle of Solidarity

Stroll through the streets of old brick houses in the harbour city of Gdansk (Danzig, pop. 466,500) when a sea breeze is blowing off the Gulf of Gdansk and you will imagine yourself back in the medieval Hanseatic era, when a commercial alliance was formed between north German cities for trade between the eastern and western sides of northern Europe. Today Gdansk looks just as it did when it was originally built by those rich merchants and ship owners: a prosperous, commercial city and port, proud of its tradition. This was the crowning achievement of the Polish restorers. During World War II the city was more or less razed to the ground, and it took until 1975 to clear all the rubble and complete the its reconstruction.

Reminder of the Hanseatic era

The Town Hall tower

History

No one knows how old this traditional city really is. All that is certain is that 'Gydanyzc' was mentioned in a document in 997 as a fortified settlement and the seat of a Slavic prince at the place where the River Motlawa flows into the Vistula just before it enters the Baltic. It received a town charter in 1326, after it had already become an international trade centre and belonged to the Hanseatic League. The fact that it had also been an object of dispute between various leaders is further evidence of the importance of Gdansk from an early stage in its history. In 1308 the Teutonic Knights took over the town and founded a new settlement on its southern boundary that later became known as Glowne Miasto, the Main Town.

After the decline of the Teutonic Knights, the independent towns united and recognised Polish sovereignty in 1454 and in its new form Gdansk was able to negotiate an autonomous status with numerous privileges. The symbiosis with Poland also brought it great prosperity, as is evident from the splendid buildings which graced the town, then the largest in Poland, in the 16th and 17th centuries.

The restored restaurant Pod Lososiem (The Salmon Restaurant) is a reminder of Gdansk's position as a trade metropolis and meeting place for merchants from all over Europe. It was for them, in 1704, that an enterprising Dutchman opened the restaurant that was to become famous from Hamburg to Novgorod, compounding its fame with the invention of 'Gdansk Goldwasser' (literally, gold water), a sweet vodka containing flakes of gold leaf that is still produced today.

Only one of the Polish kings, Stefan Batory (1575–86), attempted – unsuccessfully – to restrict the autonomy of the city. Otherwise Gdansk shared the fate of the Polish-Lithuanian monarchy, until the second partition of Poland in 1793 when it became Prussian.

From 1920 to 1939 Gdansk, together with the surrounding areas of the Vistula island, became a free city and the residence of the high commissioner of the League of Nations. World War II, which began in Gdansk, ended with disastrous consequences for the city: when in March 1945 joint units of the Red Army and the Polish army marched into the city that had been fiercely defended by the Germans to the last, 90 percent of the historic buildings had been destroyed. The events in Gdansk during World War II are vividly recreated by Günter Grass in his novel *The Tin Drum*.

Solidarnosc memorial

Shipyard cranes

Solidarity

Forty years later Gdansk once again came into the public spotlight, when Solidarity, a trade union movement against the Communist government, was formed. Gdansk shipbuilders, led by Lech Walesa, triggered public strikes in protest to massive price increases, and in 1980 an agreement was signed allowing, among other demands, Solidarity to become legal.

In the 15 months of its activity, Solidarity proved to be a peaceful reform movement which, with its 10 million members, represented the whole nation. However, on 13 December 1981, the head of the party, General Jaruzelski, proclaimed martial law. Solidarity was disbanded and its leaders imprisoned, starting a wave of repression.

The economic crisis worsened and the government proved to be unable to cope. With the leadership of Mikhail Gorbachev, the Soviet Union no longer showed any imperial tendencies and by the autumn of 1988, the party agreed to share political power. In June 1989, the first freely elected non-Communist government took power.

Sights

Walking round the reconstructed ★★ **Main Town** (Glówne Miasto) today, it is hard to believe that just under 50 years ago all this was a heap of rubble. Enter the town on the west side through the magnificent ★ **Upland Gate ❶** (Brama Wyzynna) built in 1588. This marks the start of the ★ **Royal Way**, along which the rulers formerly paraded into the town. On the other side of the ★ **Golden Gate ❷**, a splendid Manneristic construction resembling a triumphal arch, is ★ **ulica Dluga** or Long Street. Before continuing further along the Royal Way in the direction of the River Motlawa, make a detour to look at the ★ **Great Arsenal ❸** (Wielka Zbrojownia). The magnificent building, also in the Manneristic style, now houses a market. It is the work of the Dutchman Anthonis van Opbergen, an important Gdansk architect, who also built the 'Hamlet Castle' Kronborg in Helsingor, Denmark. Back on Long Street, the fine residences on either side testify to the wealth of the men who originally built them.

The Golden Gate

The ★ **Town Hall ❹** of the Main Town (Ratusz Glownego) at the end of Long Street is a Gothic brick building dating from 1600. The interior, which was restored at considerable cost and now houses the **Historical Museum of Gdansk**, is worth a visit. The so-called Red Room is the most magnificent of the rooms: the large pictures covering walls and ceiling transform the whole interior into a single work of art. Most of this is original, since the furnishings were stored outside Gdansk during the war.

The Long Market

Long Street opens out into ★★ **Long Market ❺** (Dlugi Targ), a wide street lined with attractive burghers' houses with showpiece facades from various epochs. One house in particular stands out, with windows extending the full height of the lower part of the building, which corresponds

Feeding the birds

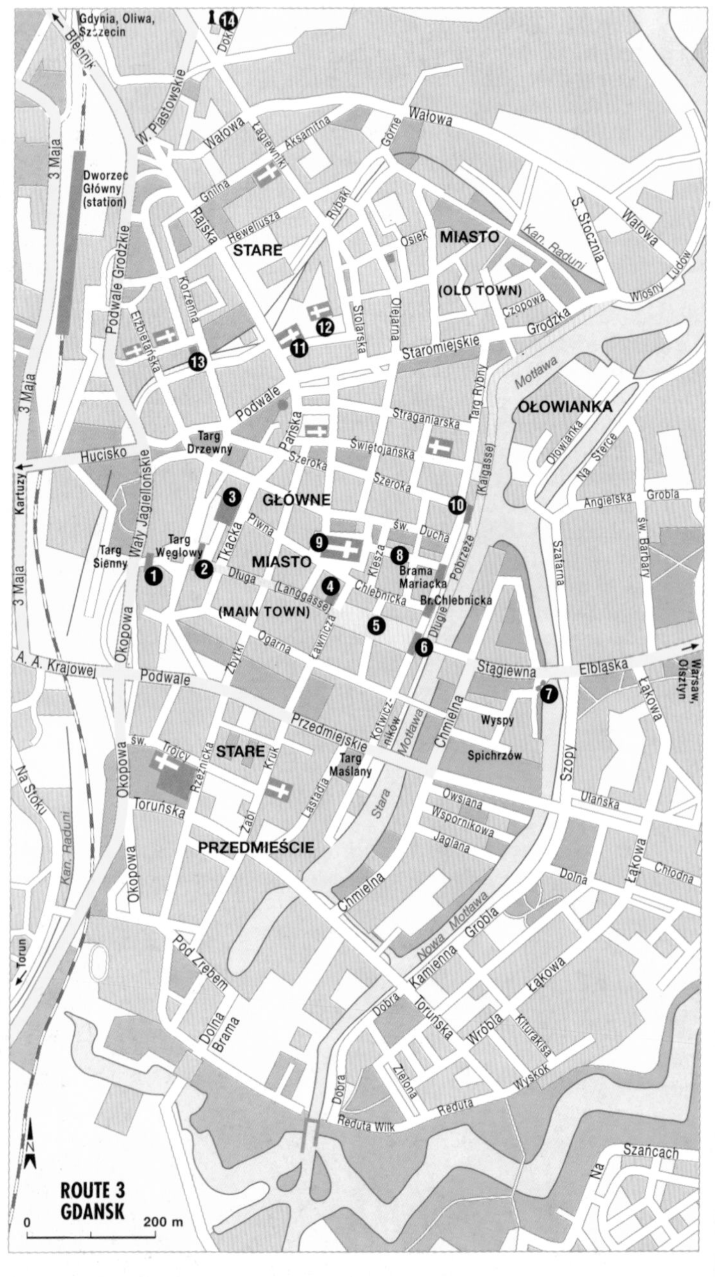

Gdynia, Oliwa, Szczecin
14
Dokk
Błędnik
W. Piastowskie
Wałowa
Łagiewniki
Aksamitna
Górne
Wałowa
3 Maja
Dworzec Główny (station)
Gnilna
Rybaki
Rajska
Heweliusza
STARE
Osiek
MIASTO
Kan. Raduni
S. Stocznia
Wałowa
Wiosny Ludów
Podwale Grodzkie
Korzenna
(OLD TOWN)
Czopowa
Grodzka
Elżbietańska
Stolarska
Olejarna
12
11
13
Staromiejskie
Motława
Targ Rybny
3 Maja
Podwale
Pańska
OŁOWIANKA
Straganiarska
Targ Drzewny
Świętojańska
Ołowianka
Na Sterce
Hucisko
Szeroka
(Kalgasse)
Kartuzy
3
GŁÓWNE
Szeroka
10
Angielska
Grobla
Piwna
św. Ducha
Targ Węglowy
9
św. Barbary
Targ Sienny
Wały Jagiellońskie
Tkacka
8
Szafarna
1
2
MIASTO
Kiesza
Brama Mariacka
Pobrzeże
3 Maja
Długa
(Langgasse)
4
Chlebnicka
Br. Chlebnicka
(MAIN TOWN)
Długie
Okopowa
5
Ogarna
6
Zbytki
Ławnicza
A. A. Krajowej
Podwale
Stągiewna
Elbląska
Warsaw, Olsztyn
7
Łąkowa
Przedmiejskie
Kotwicz-ników
Motława
Chmielna
Wyspy
św. Trójcy
STARE
Kruk
Targ Maślany
Spichrzów
Szopy
Na Stoku
Okopowa
Rzeźnicka
Stara
Ułańska
Owsiana
Toruńska
Żabi
Lastadia
Wspornikowa
Kan. Raduni
Jaglana
PRZEDMIEŚCIE
Łąkowa
Chłodna
Dolna
Okopowa
Chmielna
Nowa Motława
Grobla
Toruń
Pod Zrębem
Kamienna
Łąkowa
Dobra
Toruńska
Dolna Brama
Wróbla
Kiturakisa
Zielona
Wyskok
Dobra
Reduta
Reduta Wilk
Na Szańcach
N
ROUTE 3 GDANSK
0
200 m

to three floors of the neighbouring houses. This is **Artus Court**, which provided the appropriate framework for assemblies of the Gdansk patricians. In front of Artus Court, the 17th-century **Neptune Fountain** symbolises the importance of Gdansk as a marine power. The neighbouring **Golden House** (Zlota Kamienica) is rightly named, with a facade richly decorated with gold-plated reliefs. The **Green Gate** ❻ on the east side of Long Market marks the end of the Royal Way at the Motlawa, opposite an island containing warehouses and featuring the **Milk Churn Gate** ❼, its unusual name is derived from the shape of its round towers.

The Golden House

If a boat trip is what you have in mind, the Green Gate is also the location of the **excursion boat quay** (przystan Zielona Brama). The boat ride takes you past the wharfs and the old fortress at the mouth of the Vistula and moors by the huge monument on Westerplatte. The monument is a reminder of the outbreak of World War II, when 182 soldiers held out for seven days defending a Polish ammunition depot on the peninsula against the superior Wehrmacht.

Embark at the Green Gate

Return now to the the waterfront (Dlugie Pobrzeze), and walk north past the 15th-century Bread Gate (Brama Chlebnicka) and St Mary's Gate (Brama Mariacka), which now houses the **Archaeological Museum**. The harbour quay was always more than just the place where goods were loaded and unloaded, and today people continue to converge on it, from amber sellers, fortune-telling gypsies, German tourists in search of their roots and dubious money-changers, to boy scouts on day trips and traders selling every imaginable kind of kitsch.

On the other side of St Mary's Gate is ★ **St Mary's Street** ❽ (ulica Mariacka) leading to St Mary's Church. In front of the houses there is a row of perrons, terraces with steps leading down into the street, which were once a typical feature of towns on the Baltic coast. For the citizens of Gdansk, they were a place to see and be seen. Today they have been taken over by galleries and art shops, and were also used in the filming of *Buddenbrooks* by Thomas Mann, since no such street could be found in Lubeck, where the book is actually set.

Amber jewellery, St Mary's

★★ **St Mary's Church** ❾ is one of the largest churches in Europe with a vaulted ceiling 30m (98ft) high. This Gothic hall church was built between 1343 and 1502, and can accommodate almost 25,000 worshippers. During a fire in 1945, most of the beautiful vaulting collapsed and its reconstruction was only completed a few years ago. The massive brick building is often more of a gathering point for tourists than a place of worship. The work given

St Mary's Church detail

The Crane Gate

most attention by the guides is the triptychon *The Last Judgement* (1466–1473) by Hans Memling. The picture was commandeered by citizens of Gdansk en route to the person for whom it was painted in Tuscany and they put it up in St Mary's as war booty. What the visitor sees now however is a copy: the original is to be found in the Gdansk National Museum in the former Franciscan monastery near the Church of the Holy Trinity.

Back on the harbour promenade the next feature of interest is the 15th-century ★ **Crane Gate** ⓲ (Zuraw). The enormous harbour crane is one of the largest medieval industrial constructions in existence and now it houses a maritime museum. The Crane Gate is the symbol of Gdansk. It is typical of this trading city that it was not one of the churches but a secular building that was chosen for this honour.

St Bridget's: interior detail

A few minutes further to the north is the former **Old Town** which, by contrast with the Main Town, was not rebuilt in its original form after World War II. Jan Heweliusz, or Johannes Hevelius (1611–1686), who published one of the first detailed maps of the moon, is buried in the main church, **St Catherine's** ⓫. Since he earned little money with his astronomy, Heweliusz also worked as a brewer; today 'Hevelius' beer is as popular as ever.

The church immediately behind it, ★ **St Bridget's** ⓬, went down in recent Polish history as the 'Solidarity Church', since it was here that the anti-Communist opposition met to worship when the country was under martial law, as an expression of political disobedience. The tasteful modern interior combines surprisingly well with the reconstructed Gothic star vaults.

The tour of Gdansk ends at the **Old Town Hall** ⓭ (ratusz Starego Miasta) completed in 1595, near the main railway station.

The waterfront

Oliwa, Sopot and Gdynia

From the main station, take a taxi (or bus A, tram No 6) to the suburbs of Oliwa, Sopot and Gdynia.

A small detour in the direction of the shipyards will bring you to one of the most impressive monuments of postwar Poland: the **Monument to the Shipyard Workers** ⓮ (Pomnik Poleglyich Stoczniowcow). The three huge crosses set up near Gate 2 of the Gdansk shipyards commemorate the 28 people who died when the strike in December 1970 was suppressed. The monument was erected in 1980 by Solidarity, and when the organisation was subsequently prohibited, the Communist leaders did not dare touch the memorial because of its powerful symbolic significance.

Oliwa, today a district of Gdansk, was founded by the Cistercian order in 1188. It is famous for its ★★ **Cathedral**. Rebuilt a number of times, it dates back to the 13th century and was originally the monastery church. The interior, 100m (328ft) long, is of massive proportions. The unique acoustics, derived from the length and narrowness of the building are convincingly demonstrated when the splendid baroque ★ **organ** is played; short recitals are given regularly during the day. This 18th-century instrument has 7,876 pipes and a number of mechanised figures which move when the organ is played. An international organ festival is held in Oliva every August.

Wedding at the Cathedral

★ **Sopot**, close to Oliwa, was once one of the most fashionable sea resorts and spas in the German Reich. The villas, which are now showing their age, reflect the former lifestyle of the upper classes. It is still possible to stroll along the pier that extends 500m (1,640ft) out into the Baltic, and in the casino of the Grand Hotel wealthy night owls can indulge their passion for gambling. But the 'good old days' in Sopot will not return until the Gulf of Gdansk is clean enough to swim in once more.

Sopot Pier

Gdynia, the next town, sharply contrasts with the villa suburb of Sopot. The city – now the industrial quarter of the Tri-city – developed between the wars as a Polish port in competition with the Free City of Gdansk, which was not then part of Poland. Moored at the pier is the old battleship *Blyskawica*, which is now a museum ship, and the famous sailing-school ship *Dar Pomorza*, a three-master launched in Hamburg in 1909.

A statue of Joseph Conrad, whose real name was Jozef Korzeniowski, looks out to sea with evident longing: with this monument, Gdynia pays tribute to the great English author of Polish origin, who wrote *Lord Jim* and other stories of the sea.

The masts of the 'Dar Pomorza'

Malbork Castle

Warsaw
POLAND

Route 4

Eastwards to the Masurian Lakes

★★★ Gdansk – ★★★ Malbork – Elblag – Olsztyn – Mragowo – Gizycko – ★ Mikolajki – Lake Luknajno (416km/260 miles) *See maps on pages 24–5 and 42*

Crystal-clear lakes, unspoilt forests and the occasional village in a clearing – this is what holidaymakers who want to get away from it all are looking for. However, even in Masuria the reality may be a little different, since Poland's 'green lung' is also threatened by environmental problems. But they are nothing like as serious as those in other parts of the country, and the natural beauties of what is the most popular holiday region of Poland continue to be well worth a trip. For anglers, hikers and water-sports enthusiasts, especially canoeists, this – the 'land of a thousand lakes' – is the perfect place.

Paradise for anglers

Allow around seven days for this route which leads through Malbork (Marienburg) and Elblag (Elbing) to Olsztyn in the historic region of Warmia and from here further into the heart of the Masurian Lake District in the Mikolajki region. The most convenient form of transport for this route is obviously a car, but if you have the energy – and naturally the time – the best way to see the region is by bicycle: Masuria is a cyclists' paradise.

Many places in Masuria have good tourist facilities, even though there are not quite enough beds of Western standards in hotels during the holiday season. However, the most appropriate form of accommodation on this trip is a tent, which is not only cheap but the best way to experience the natural beauty of countryside.

From Gdansk take the E75 south on 58km (36 miles) to **Malbork** or Marienburg (pop. 40,000). The name is associated with one of the most famous buildings in Europe ★★★ **Malbork Castle** (daily 8.30am–4.30pm, grounds open until 6pm, in winter until 3pm, buildings closed on Monday). The huge fortress of the Teutonic Knights, the German name of which is Marienburg, clings like a massive red brick dragon to the steep banks of the River Nogat; the sheer scale of it takes your breath away.

Teutonic stronghold

The **Teutonic Knights** were a military order of German knights who served in the Holy Land. They played an important part in Polish history, originally acquiring their prosperity through gifts of land for their hospital work during the Crusades. They were also given land in northeast Poland in 1225 in return for assisting King Konrad III to repel an invasion of pagan Prussians. From here they gradually extended their territory, finally transferring the seat of the Grand Master from Venice to Malbork. They then spread to the west bank of the Vistula, under the continuing pretext of Christianisation, until their incursions were finally resisted by the joint Polish-Lithuanian government and they were defeated in 1410 at the legendary Battle of Grunwald. Malbork was taken over by the Poles in 1457 and the Grand Master swore allegiance to the Polish king.

The complex, which dates from the 13th and 14th centuries, is entered through the Lower Castle, which incorporates the arsenal and St Lawrence Chapel. In the adjoining Middle Castle is the **palace of the Grand Master** – later used occasionally as a residence by the Polish king and his governors – the Great Refectory (at present inaccessible) and the rooms formerly used for the knight's guests. A bridge leads across to the High Castle where the knights themselves lived. Together with the chapter hall, the castle's church will be one of the most outstanding features when restoration work has been completed. For the moment visitors have to content themselves with the **Golden Gate**, the doorway of the church, which is richly decorated with mythical beasts.

A tower, which is connected to the castle by a passage can be seen off to the side of the complex near the river. This is the Gdanisko Tower which, for those less well versed in medieval castle architecture, was simply a large toilet, hence its position not within the walls but at a discreet 'safe distance' outside. Here the Nogat functioned as the natural sewerage system.

The only way to see around the castle is by joining one of the lengthy guided tours. In the west wing of the **Middle Castle** is a permanent exhibition on the origins and processing of amber. Many visitors will be surprised to discover that 'Baltic gold' is nothing more than fossilised resin from conifers dating back to the Eocene epoch.

Made into valuable jewellery, it brought great prosperity to the coastal towns. Today amber jewellery is one of the most popular souvenirs from Poland.

From across the river, lit by the afternoon sun, Malbork Castle is a fantastic sight.

Elblag, or Elbing (pop. 120,000; 100km/60 miles) from Malbork is situated on the Baltic coast. Because of its ideal location, the town has changed hands several times over the centuries, and was often destroyed by the victors in the process. Pagan Prussians and German knights, Prussians and Poles, Swedes and Russians all coveted the Baltic port, and at the end of World War II Elblag was nothing but a heap of rubble.

Elblag and the famous canal

Although it is being rebuilt – around 50 houses in the Old Town are to be reconstructed in their original form on the basis of historic documents, while the rest will be in post-modern style – it will be a long time before its former importance as a port is re-established. For 40 years the harbour could not be used: the only exit to the Baltic from the Vistula Lagoon (Zalew Wislany) was at the Russian town of Baltijsk, access to which was prohibited by the Baltic fleet stationed there. As a result, Elblag could not be reached by water. The hydrofoils that now ply between Elblag and Kaliningrad have in the meantime become a popular tourist attraction.

Elblag is best known for the ★★ **Kanal Ostrodzko-Elblaski** (trips along this 80-km/50-mile waterway to Ostroda start during the season from Elblag at 8am). Built in 1858, the canal is the only one in the world where the ships travel overland as well as on the water. This marvel of technology covers a height difference of almost 100m (328ft) and includes so-called inclined planes, used to haul boats overland on trolleys.

The little town of **Frombork**, 32km (20 miles) north of Elblag on the Vistula Lagoon, is well worth a detour. It boasts a 14th-century ★★ **Cathedral** perched on a hill and surrounded by well-fortified walls and towers. Its distinctive form with its ornate facade, flanked by two slim towers, is best viewed from one of the fortified towers, which also provide a splendid view of the lagoon and the spit of land on the other side.

Continue to **Paslek** (pop. 10,000; 122km/76 miles). Dutch colonists developed this area in the 14th century by building dams and applying successful drainage techniques. Fill your picnic basket at Paslek's well-stocked delicatessens, ready for a picnic by the canal (follow the sign marked 'Sluza Buczyniec 8km' on the outskirts of the town, behind the new petrol station). Have your cameras ready at 12.20pm to capture a picture of a vessel being hauled overland.

Drive through the village of Drulity to Morzewo and return to the E77 which will bring you in no time to **Ostroda** (pop. 35,000), the starting point for canoe tours.

The next stop is **Grunwald** (200km/125 miles), Poland's most famous battlefield. On 15 July 1410 the combined Polish-Lithuanian army inflicted a crushing defeat on the troops of the Teutonic Knights in the Battle of Grunwald, one of the biggest battles in the Middle Ages. Today a monument erected in 1960 commemorates this key event in Polish history.

The history trail continues in nearby **Olsztynek** (pop. 15,000; 226km/141 miles), whose main attraction is the ★ **open-air museum** (*skansen*). Set in beautiful countryside are examples of old peasants' houses from Masuria and Warmia. The museum is at the northeastern exit of the town so there is no need to leave the route to Olsztyn.

Although **Olsztyn** (pop. 150,000; 251km/156 miles), is surrounded by a belt of modern housing and industrial estates, the reconstructed ★ **Old Town** has provided artists and craftsmen with an attractive setting for their studios and galleries, which attract many visitors.

After a walk around the Old Town, time should be left for a visit to the 14th-century ★ **Castle** (*zamek*), which now houses the **Museum of Warmia and Masuria** with its art and natural science collections. The unusual stone figures standing in the castle courtyard are idols once worshipped by the pagan Prussians and date from the early Middle Ages. They are all that has remained of the people to whom this country once belonged.

The ★ **Parish Church of St James** (Kosciol Sw Jakuba) was built at the same time as the castle. The most outstanding feature of this church is the Gothic star and net vaulting which elegantly patterns the ceiling. Olsztyn's modern attraction is the **Copernicus Planetarium** in the aleja Zwyciestwa, where outer space is shown not from the perspective of the Earth's inhabitants but from that of the astronauts (Tuesday to Friday 10.30am–6pm).

The beauty of the Masurian countryside can be enjoyed from the road, from the deck of the excursion steamers on nearby Lake Ukiel or from the air. A bird's-eye view of Masuria is offered by the Aeroklub, ul. Sielska 34, tel: 0048-89 27 52 40 and Air Touristik, ul. Lotnicza 1, tel: 0048-89 27 20 15. The airfield is in Dajtki on the western edge of town (on national highway 16).

On a rainy day in this natural paradise, an excursion to the ★ **Lidzbark Warminski Castle**, just under 50km (31 miles) north of Olsztyn, will distract attention from the grey skies. The residence of the Warmian bishops was built

Monument to a fierce battle

Olsztynek: open-air museum

Olsztyn Castle

Lake Ukiel

Lidzbark Warminski Castle

Sorkwity village church

after 1350; next to Malbork Castle it is the most impressive building in the region. The excellently preserved rooms feature fine vaulting and original wall paintings.

From Olsztyn the route follows national highway 16 in an easterly direction. Make the most of this attractive stretch of road and take time to stop off in one of the many picturesque spots en route. After 50km (31 miles) you will arrive at **Sorkwity** (pop. 900; 301km/188 miles), and shortly after entering the village you will see the whitewashed ★ **village church** on the left-hand side of the road, one of the few Protestant churches in Masuria today. The pastor, who lives opposite, will gladly open the church and point out its proudest possession, a colourful baptismal angel hovering high above the heads of the faithful near the ceiling of the nave. With the help of a block and tackle construction the wooden sculpture can be lowered at christenings and the head of the child being christened is moistened with holy water from the silver dish it holds.

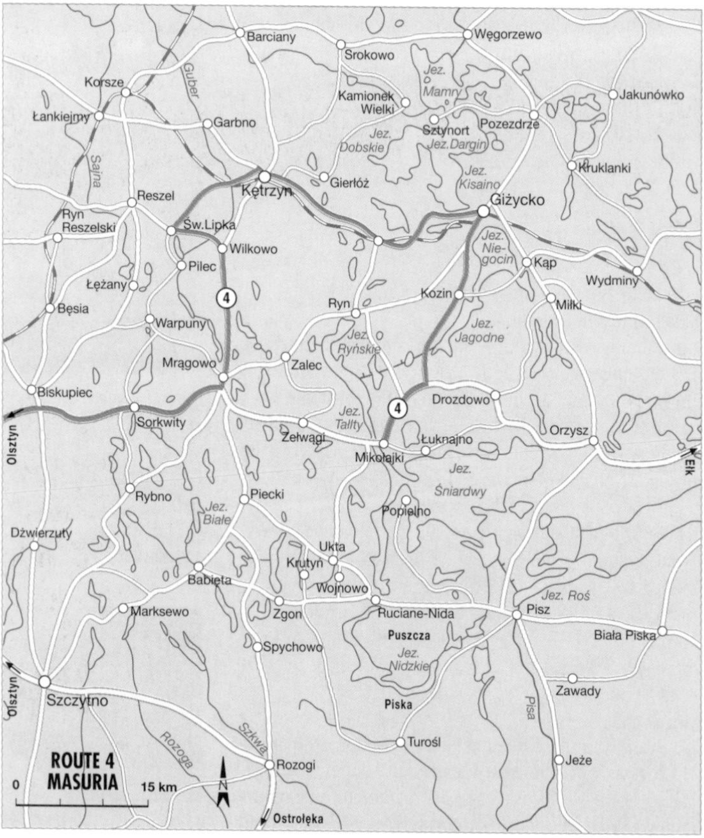

ROUTE 4 MASURIA

The organ at Swieta Lipka

★ **Sorkwity Palace**, a picture-book palace in 19th-century 'neoTudor' style, is set in appropriately enchanting surroundings in the midst of old oak trees on the shore of Lake Lampackie.

Further along the route lies **Mragowo** (pop. 21,000; 313km/196 miles), nestling in beautiful countryside. And since from here the classic tourist attractions such as Swieta Lipka and the largest of the Masurian Lakes can be reached in a day, the owners of hotels and guesthouses can never complain of a shortage of guests.

Sorkwity Palace

A must on every tour of Masuria is a visit to the place of pilgrimage **Swieta Lipka** (literally the Holy Lime Tree). The 15-km (9-mile) trip over moraines and along the shores of beautiful lakes is in itself very worthwhile. Hikers staying in Mragowo will want to take the 22-km (14-mile) trail that leads to Swieta Lipka where the 17th-century ★★ **pilgrimage church**, a splendid ochre-coloured Baroque building with two towers and a facade ornamented with columns and sculptures, stands in a large clearing. Every hour the **18th-century organ** is played, setting in motion the small biblical figures that are attached to the instrument. Swieta Lipka is one of the most popular sights in Masuria, so it is seldom the place suitable for quiet meditation often expected of a church of pilgrimage.

It is only a 14km (9 miles) from here to **Ketrzyn** (349km/218 miles), famous for a collection of buildings constructed for a very specific purpose: a few kilometres to the east, near the village of Gierloz in the middle of the Masurian woods, is a huge bunker complex constructed out of tons of steel and concrete that was once the headquarters of Adolf Hitler, the 'Wolf's Lair'. For two years with only short interruptions, Hitler occupied this compound, directing much of his war strategy from here. It was here, on 20 July 1944, that Klaus Graf Schenk von

Hitler's bunker at Ketrzyn

The scene of the failed attempt

Stauffenberg exploded a bomb in a courageous, though unsuccessful, assassination attempt on Hitler; the 'Fuhrer', however, was elsewhere at the time.

Today it is a very popular tourist attraction, although one does not have to be particularly sensitive to find the massive ruin oppressive. At the kiosk there is a plan of the complex and local guides are available.

The ★★ **Masurian landscape** is made up of thousands of lakes and majestic hills. In the rushes along the banks of the lakes, swans, cranes, herons, crested divers and ducks find safe nesting places. The waters are teeming with eels, pike and salmon trout.

Gizycko (pop. 28,000; 381km/238 miles) is the most popular holiday centre in Masuria. It is in an idyllic location between two lakes: Lake Niegocin in the south and Lake Kisajno in the north, which is actually part of Lake Mamry. In 1772 a canal was built between the two lakes, a route which today is used almost exclusively by water-sports enthusiasts. Excursion boats are perhaps a safer way of enjoying the scenery for the less actively inclined, and are certainly a more tranquil alternative, connecting the town with Mikolajki (4½ hours) and Wegorzewo (2½ hours).

Farming country near Mikolajki

★ **Mikolajki** (pop. 4,000; 416km/260 miles) is somewhat exaggeratedly called 'Masurian Venice'. It is, however, a particularly beautiful town, and in the holiday season the tourists are in the majority, as they have been for the last 100 years. Close to the largest Masurian lake, Lake Sniardwy, it is an Eldorado for nature lovers and water-sports fans. Excursion boats leave from Mikolajki for trips on the big lakes.

An interesting point at which to end this tour of Masuria may be **Lake Luknajno**, 5km (3 miles) east of Mikolajki. The lake is the home of thousands of wild swans and herons every summer, and they can be observed from an observation centre.

Lake Luknajo

Krutyn, a small place near Ukta south of Mikolajki, is situated on what is probably the most picturesque river in Masuria, the Krutynia, and has long been well-known among canoeists. The ★★ **punting trips** organised from Krutyn are to be greatly recommended. Leave the punting to the local boatman and sit back and enjoy this splendid waterway. The green tunnel and the shimmering red stones over which the crystal-clear water of the river flows, and the peace and quiet broken only by the gliding of the boat will long be your best memory of Masuria.

To the southeast lies the **Puszcza Piska**, a wilderness of primeval fir and pine forest supporting a variety of wildlife including wild boar and bison.

Market day in Chelmno

Route 5

Along the Vistula

★★★ Gdansk – ★★ Chelmno – ★★ Torun – ★ Plock – ★★★ Warsaw (406km/254 miles) *See map on pages 24–5*

This route follows Poland's most famous river, the Vistula. It leads from Gdansk to Warsaw, passing through places of great historic significance such as Torun. It is a journey through the 1,000-year history and culture of the country, with the capital of Poland undoubtedly the high point of the trip, and is designed to take three days. The journey begins in Gdansk (*see pages 31–7*).

Grudziadz: granary detail

Outside ★ **Gniew**, which has the remains of a Teutonic Knights' castle, is the old Cistercian abbey of **Pelplin**, only 4km (2½ miles) from the main road. The severe-looking exterior of the ★ **Abbey church**, dating from the 14th century, contrasts sharply with the interior, which has a fine ceiling with elaborate net-vaulting.

In just under an hour's drive further on, there is a fine panoramic view of old **Grudziadz** (pop. 100,000; 113km/71 miles) on the other side of the Vistula. Since the construction of the Prussian fortress here in 1786, Grudziadz has remained a military town. The buildings fronting the river for which the town is famous are a complex of 26 granaries dating from the 16th to 18th centuries.

Sunflower season

What is probably the most attractive part of this route now continues through lush meadows on the east bank of the Vistula. Take time over this section and stop and take a walk down to the river, as it is no great distance to the medieval town of ★★ **Chelmno** (pop. 22,000; 145km/91 miles), the next stop. Chelmno is a must for anyone interested in Polish history.

Chelmno had its heyday between the 13th and 15th centuries when it belonged to the Hanseatic League (*see Route 3, page 31*). Before exploring the ★★ **Old Town** perched on the high banks of the Vistula and visible from a long way away, it is worth gathering some background information about the city's past in the **Regional Museum**. This is located in the **Town Hall** on the market square, a 16th-century building in the Italian Renaissance style and the northernmost example of this type of architecture, which spread here via Cracow. What is unusual about it is its structure, with a large, ornamented attic and windows which diminish in size towards the bottom of the building, literally turning the ancient theory of proportions on its head. **St Mary's Church**, on the market square with its distinctive outline, was built from 1290–1333 and features Gothic frescoes in the choir and the figures of 11 apostles on the pillars. The Old Town is completely surrounded by the city wall, which dates from the 14th century. Several bastions and the Grudiadz Gate (Brama Grudiadzka) have remained, showing the layout of the medieval town.

Chelmno Town hall

The route leaves the Vistula for a short time and takes the direct route on the E75. The river makes a detour, curving west, where it skirts the large industrial town of Bydgoszcz, which has little to offer in the way of attractions.

Quite the opposite, however, is true of ★★ **Torun** (pop. 205,000; 190km/119 miles), which boasts an ensemble of Gothic architecture that is unique in Europe. In the year 1233 the Teutonic Knights founded a castle on the banks of the Vistula which functioned as a centre for operations against the Prussians. For a time Torun belonged to the Hanseatic League and had trading partners as far away as Holland. The pressure put on by the merchants of Torun for greater independence soon brought them into conflict

Torun: fresco in St John's Church

with the authoritarian overlords at the castle. In 1455 the conflict came to a head and ended with the citizens of Torun storming the stronghold of the Teutonic Knights and destroying it completely. The city then acknowledged the sovereignty of the Polish king but was astute enough to negotiate its own autonomy.

The buildings of the ★★ **Old Town** are concentrated into a small space. The old market square is dominated by the ★ **Town Hall**, which has survived through the centuries intact. The massive brick building originates from the 13th century and was enlarged at a later stage to give it its present form with four wings. It now provides a fine setting for the **Regional Museum**.

Statue of Copernicus

In front of the Town Hall is the **statue of Copernicus**. The great astronomer Nicholas Copernicus (1473–1543) is Torun's most famous son and is still celebrated in Poland as one of history's greatest scientists. The nearby **Copernicus Museum**, ul. Kopernica 17, furnishes the proof: the 15th-century building where Copernicus is said to have been born houses a comprehensive collection of exhibits relating to him, including the original edition of *De revolutionibus orbium Coelestium* (1543). With this book Copernicus refuted the Church's doctrine that the earth was the centre of the universe.

On the east side of the Old Market Square is a patrician house dating from 1697, the House under the Star (Dom pod Gwiazda), which is now the **Museum of Far Eastern Art**. A few paces away in the direction of the Vistula, the massive tower of ★ **St John's Church** is impossible to overlook. The church with its three distinctive roofs dates from the 14th century; the famous *Beautiful Madonna* on the north wall of the apse is only a copy of the original statue, which disappeared during the war, but the early Gothic frescoes in the choir have been preserved in their original form.

The Old Town has two other churches, each of a quite different character: the baroque Church of the Holy Spirit (1754–56) with its 64-m (210-ft) tower and **St Mary's Church** (after 1351), a Gothic building which, in accordance with the regulations of the Franciscan order, has no tower at all. The outstanding features of St Mary's are the beautiful frescoes on the south wall – the church seems very high because of the narrowness of the naves – and the Manneristic sarcophagi of members of the Torun nobility in the southern nave.

Ciechocinek: on top of the tower

Cross back over the Vistula and drive a further 22km (14 miles) on the E75 to ★★ **Ciechocinek**. The main attraction of this spa is the graduation tower dating from 1828, said to be the oldest and largest in the world. Today it is no longer used for extracting salt, but fulfils a therapeu-

Growing up in Wloclawek

tic function: the air in its vicinity has a high salt and mineral content which has a beneficial effect on those suffering from respiratory diseases and is also said to increase general wellbeing.

The climate of **Wloclawek** (pop. 110,000; 246km/154 miles) is anything but beneficial. The industrial metropolis with its paper and china factories, which discharge their waste water into the Vistula, is largely responsible for the catastrophic state of the river. Wloclawek is nevertheless worth visiting for its **cathedral**. Begun in the 14th century, the church houses the marble sarcophagus of Bishop Piotr of Bnin, which was the work of the Nuremberg artist Veit Stoss in 1493.

Industry rules

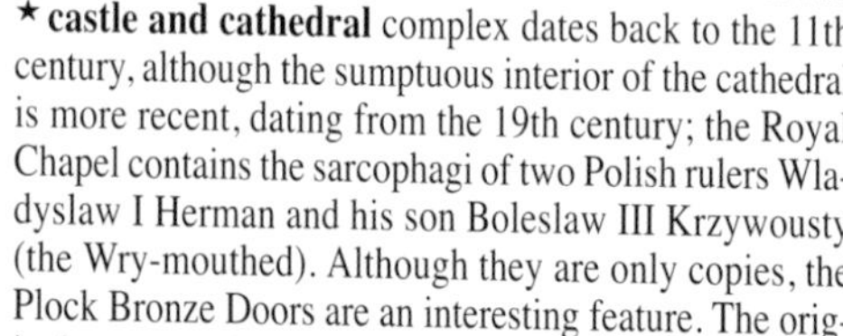

Shortly before Warsaw, make a final stop in ★ **Plock** (pop. 135,000; 296km/185 miles). Plock is not only an important centre of the oil industry, it also attracts many tourists with its castle perched on the cliff above the Vistula. The ★ **castle and cathedral** complex dates back to the 11th century, although the sumptuous interior of the cathedral is more recent, dating from the 19th century; the Royal Chapel contains the sarcophagi of two Polish rulers Wladyslaw I Herman and his son Boleslaw III Krzywousty (the Wry-mouthed). Although they are only copies, the Plock Bronze Doors are an interesting feature. The originals were made for Plock in the 12th century in Magdeburg but, as a result of a mysterious conflict, they found their way to Russia where, as the Novgorod Bronze Doors, they embellish the Cathedral of St Sophia.

In the castle, once the seat of the Mazovian dukes, the **Art Nouveau Collection** (Muzeum Mazowieckie, zbyory Secesji) of crafts, furniture and paintings is the best of its kind in Poland.

Plock: cathedral statue

Warsaw (*see page 16*) is a further 110km (68 miles).

Route 6

The cradle of the Polish state

★★★ Warsaw – Gniezno – ★★ Poznan – ★ Lagow (522km/326 miles) *See map on pages 50–1*

This route runs in more or less a straight line from east to west, taking in Gniezno, a city which goes back 1,000 years, and Poznan, a city second to Warsaw in industrial and cultural stature. It ends in the idyllic countryside on the eastern border of Germany. Three days should be allowed in all. Finding hotel rooms may be a problem, especially when a fair is on in Poznan, so it is advisable to make reservations in advance. The journey begins in Warsaw.

After 77km (48 miles) take the left-hand turning to ★ **Nieborow**. The baroque palace of Nieborow is a highly typical example of early 18th-century architecture and was designed by Tylman van Gameren. It belonged to the Radziwills, a rich Polish-Lithuanian aristocratic family, until 1945 and is surrounded by extensive gardens. The palace has a comprehensive collection of *objets d'art* rather eccentrically arranged with antique sculptures next to fine handicraft exhibits. Among the sculptures dotted around the beautiful park is the *Stone Women*, brought from the steppes on the shores of the Baltic Sea.

Arcadia sunset

The name of the next village ★★ **Arcadia**, is in itself sufficient to awaken feelings of longing. In fact, it owes its existence to the longing of one woman, Helena Radizwill, for the legendary Arcadia, which motivated her to create her own private paradise on this spot. The picturesque landscaped garden with its artificial ponds and stream has its own special charm and the picture is completed by a neoclassical Temple of Diana, an aqueduct and the 'House of the High Priest'.

If at all possible, try to time your visit to ★ **Lowicz** (pop. 30,000; 91km/57 miles) so that you arrive there for Corpus Christi. The town is renowned for its traditional colourful procession on the feast day, which usually falls around the beginning of June, when the people of Lowicz proudly present themselves in their famous national costumes.

Regional Museum and entrance sign

An old trading city, Lowicz is known for its traditional folk arts and crafts. The wood carvings, silhouettes and brightly coloured handwoven materials of Lowicz are much in demand all over the country. The ethnographic section of the ★ **Regional Museum** has a comprehensive collection of exhibits illustrating the customs and traditional crafts of the region, including artistic papercuts. The museum is housed in the former Missionary College, a baroque building in the town centre. The **Collegiate**

The Collegiate Church

Church dating from 1668 is worth a visit for its rich baroque decoration and the Old Town still has numerous historic burghers' houses from the 18th and 19th centuries.

In the village of **Ladek**, west of Konin (218km/136 miles), is a particularly beautiful monastery set in picturesque countryside by the Warta. ★ **Lad Monastery** should on no account be missed: founded in 1175 by Cistercian monks, it was repeatedly extended and reconstructed over the following six centuries. The present abbey church is predominantly baroque.

The route now continues via side roads, first in a northerly direction to ★★ **Gniezno** (pop. 70,000; 285km/178 miles), which is an absolute must on your trip.

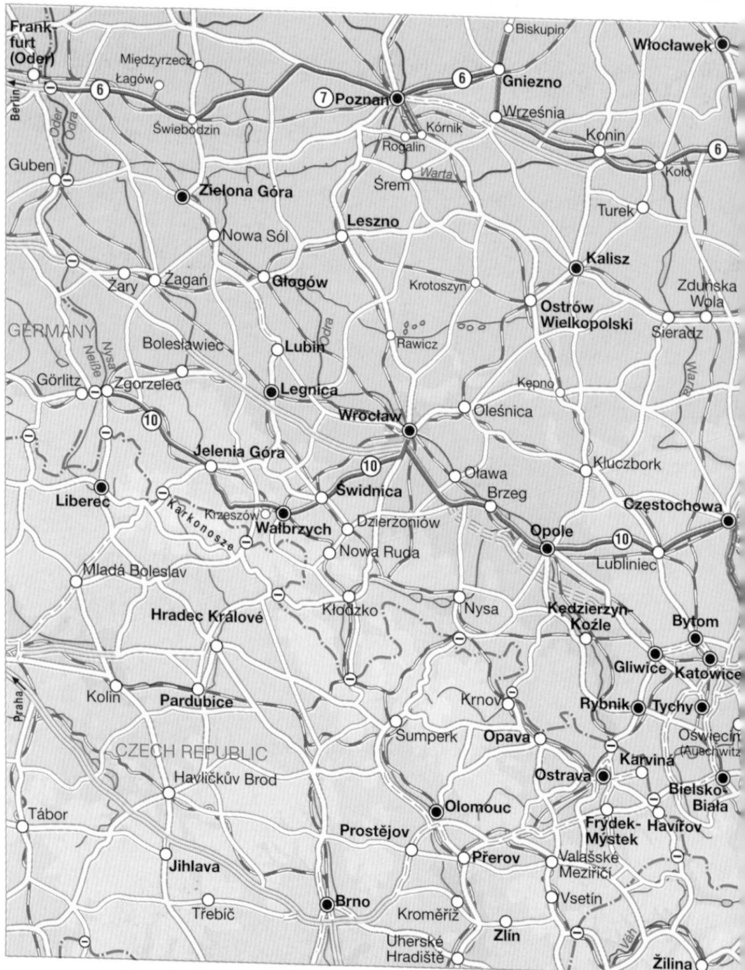

Gniezno was the first capital of the Kingdom of Poland, and it is now almost 1,000 years ago that the German Emperor Otto III and Boleslaw I Chrobry (the Brave) met here. On that occasion, Otto not only sanctioned the establishment of the archbishopric of Gniezno but also promised to support the coronation of Boleslaw as king of the new state of Poland.

The 14th-century ★★ **Cathedral** still dominates the town, which was been built on hills. The most monumental Gothic 'temple' in all Poland, outstanding among the cathedral's treasures are the Romanesque bronze doors (in the western part of the south nave), dating from 1170, which were probably cast in Liège workshops. On the doors are reliefs illustrating the life of St Adalbert (Woj-

Gniezno Cathedral

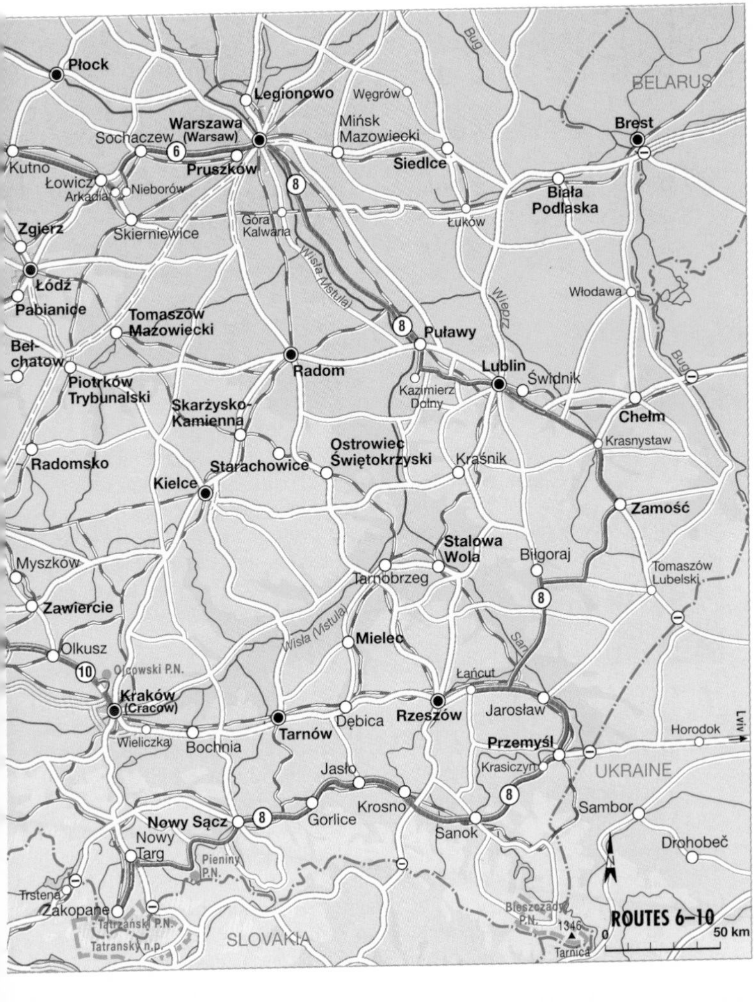

Biskupin bee hives

ciech in Polish), who ranks alongside St Stanislaus as the most important saint in Poland as well as in Bohemia. In 18 scenes, the Prague bishop Adalbert is depicted leaving Gniezno in 997 to go to the pagan Prussians, baptising them, celebrating mass and preaching and then finally being killed by them with axes and spears, after which the later King Boleslaw Chrobry is shown buying his body for its weight in gold. St Adalbert is buried in a silver sarcophagus in the centre of the main nave.

Biskupin: the fortified village

The next stop, **Biskupin**, will take you even further back in history. The village, 38km (24 miles) north of Gniezno, is famous for its archaelogical findings, which date back to the 6th century BC. In the Iron Age a tribe of a vanished culture, the Lusatian culture, built a ★ **fortified village** on an island in Lake Biskupin that in the course of time has become a peninsula. The settlement has been partially reconstructed.

To get to ★★ **Poznan** (*see pages 53–6*) from Biskupin either take the E261 via Gniezno or, if you have a good map and competent navigator, follow the road that leads to the city through attractive villages.

Smiles from Swiebodzin

A wide road leads west from Poznan in the direction of the German border. **Swiebodzin**, 122km (76 miles) from Poznan lies in the former region of Neumark. To appreciate the charms of this part of Poland, a stop at ★ **Lagow** (pop. 6,000; 468km/292 miles) is recommended. This classic resort, 50km (30 miles) from Frankfurt-on-Oder on the German border, is splendidly located between Lake Lagowskie and Lake Ciecz, and is very popular with holidaymakers. The tower of the **castle** built by the Knights of St John is visible from afar; dating from the 14th century it is surrounded by forbidding defensive walls. A small hotel is located in the castle.

Route 7

★★ Poznan – the heart of Poland

The industrial centre and trade fair city of Poznan (pop. 589,700) is the most important city in western Poland after Warsaw from an economic, cultural and historical point of view. The area around Poznan, Wielkopolska (Great Poland), is regarded as the heart of the Polish state.

Gnomes near Poznan

History

The favourable position of Poznan on the River Warta, astride the legendary Amber Road between the Baltic Coast and the Mediterranean, which was well-travelled even in the Middle Ages, was responsible for its development as a trade metropolis. The city's tradition as a trade fair centre goes back to the 15th century, when several business-minded citizens got together and organised the first official fair; soon this event was well-known in the relevant circles and its fame spread to as far away as the Far East.

Poznan has had a hard time during its long history trying to establish a reputation as the political and cultural centre that it has in fact always been, so pronounced was its image as a city of shopkeepers.

In the 19th century it became part of the Prussian state, and Prussian virtues came to be attributed to the Polish citizens of Poznan, who were thus said to be efficient and reliable but not very hospitable and rather lacking in imagination. However, the city played a major part in the

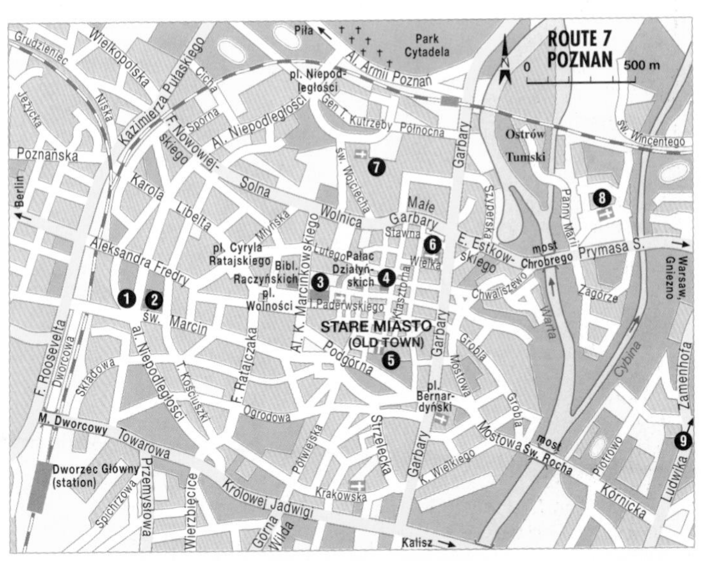

Monument to Polish resistance

Polish independence movement, which was repeated later in the struggles for liberation from the Nazis. During World War II, nearly half the city was destroyed but reconstruction proceeded rapidly and the pre-war population figures were quickly doubled.

Sights

Leaving the exhibition centre to the west of the city centre and entering the historic heart of Poznan, the first thing you encounter is the **Monument to the Victims of June 1956** ❶, a reminder of recent history when the workers went on strike in protest against the Communist government. Opposite the monument is the massive grey bulk of the **Palace of Culture** ❷, the former residence of Wilhelm II in the neo-Romanesque palace style. In spite of its rather off-putting appearance, it is worth investigating as it almost always has interesting exhibitions on a wide variety of subjects.

The main shopping street, Swiety Marcin, has all the atmosphere of a lively, modern big city. From here art lovers can direct their steps into the ★ **National Museum** ❸ (Muzeum Narodwe). Its comprehensive collections cover ethnography, city history and arts and crafts, but the collection most worth seeing comprises paintings by old Polish and West European masters. The collection, which is one of the best in Poland, includes works by Ribera, Zurbaran, Bellini and Bronzino.

Diagonally opposite, on the Plac Wolnosci, is the imposing **Raczynski Library** with its magnificent neoclassical facade featuring 24 Corinthian columns (1829). The library is a monument to the largely trouble-free coexis-

Transport in the Market Square

tence of the Poles and Germans at the beginning of the 19th century, which came to an end in the following decades with the growing insistence on Germanisation. Walking past the **Dzialynski Palace**, a 1773 burgher's house that is an unusual mixture of late baroque and neoclassical styles, you arrive at the delightful ★ **Old Market Square** ❹, where the finest building is unquestionably the ★★ **Town Hall**, an excellent example of secular Polish-Italian architecture. It was rebuilt in the 16th century, when it acquired its present elegant Renaissance form. Its most striking feature is its complex main facade embellished with sgraffito decoration, which consists of three floors of arcaded loggias topped by a high attic. Inside is the **Historical Museum of Poznan**: perhaps even more interesting than the exhibits, however, are the Renaissance rooms with their original interiors, including the splendid Great Hall with a coffered ceiling that rests on only two pillars.

The Town Hall

The **Archaeological Museum** near the Old Market Square (ulica Klasztorna 14) ranges from the Stone Age to the late Middle Ages. It is the second oldest museum in Poland and is housed in one of the excellently restored burgher's houses of the old town.

Close to the museum, in ulica Golebia, is the ★ **Parish Church of Poznan** ❺ (Kosciol Farny), built by the Jesuits in the second half of the 17th century. Massive pillars which, in accordance with the illusionistic style of the baroque era have no supporting function, dominate the interior of the church.

Poznan's parish church

Of the numerous other churches in the city, the former **Dominican Church** ❻ in ulica Dominikanska is particularly worth a visit. Although it was rebuilt in the baroque style, the church still has a fine brick portal dating from the 13th century. It was the Dominicans who brought the techniques of Gothic brick architecture from Italy to Poland before the German Gothic style took over in Pomerania and in Prussia, where the order originated.

It is worth taking the trouble to visit **St Adalbert's Church** ❼ (Kosciol Sw. Wojciecha) a little further out of the centre. Perched on a hill and recognisable by its wooden bell tower, it does not look very special, but is important to the citizens of Poznan, primarily as the burial place of many famous people, including Jozef Wybicki (1747–1822), the composer of the Polish national anthem.

The Cathedral – a national shrine

Now cross the Warta to the ★ **Cathedral** ❽. Cathedral Island (Ostrow Tumski), no longer so much an island as the arm of the river, has gradually narrowed and is the location of several historic buildings. The cathedral is already almost a Polish national shrine, since this is the burial place of the nation's founder, Mieszko I. His mausoleum and that of his successor, Boleslaw Chrobry I, are

The Golden Chapel

in the **Golden Chapel**, a 19th-century addition in neo-Byzantine style. The cathedral is in fact a jigsaw of different styles: Ottonian, Romanesque, Gothic, Renaissance, baroque and neoclassical.

After so much culture and history, it is time for a break, and this last stop on your tour of the city is conveniently close to **Lake Maltanskie** ❾ where welcome refreshment can be obtained in the beer garden.

Excursions

Instead of heading west out of Poznan straight away (*see page 52*), it is worth spending a day visiting the area to the south of the city.

Girls about town

Kornik

Kornik (pop. 8,000) is only 20km (12 miles) away and the first thing you see is the castle located on the shore of a lake. ★ **Kornik Castle** is new by Polish standards, originating from the beginning of the 18th century; in the first half of the 19th century it was redesigned in English neo-Gothic style, a project in which the German architect Karl Friedrich Schinkel was involved. The adjoining arboretum, influenced by English landscape gardening traditions, is an extensive park said to contain over 3,000 species of exotic trees from all over the world. The art collection includes everything that one might expect to find in a 'real' castle: armour, oriental weapons and precious craft work.

Kornik: the Aboretum

Rogalin

Only 13km (8 miles) further on, this village, situated on the River Warta, also has a beautiful park with another prestigious residence built by Polish aristocrats. The ★ **Palace of the Raczynski family**, a fine piece of neoclassical architecture, is open to the public and has an interesting clock collection. A gallery exhibiting excellent Polish and Western European paintings and a fine collection of old coaches are accommodated in pavilions adjacent to the palace.

While the aristocrats of Kornik were influenced by English garden traditions, the owners of Rogalin favoured the French style. The park merges with an oak forest, which has the greatest number of oak trees of any forest in Europe. In the park itself are three oak trees which are 800 years old – the oldest and largest in Europe. They have been named after the three founders of the Slavic nations, Lech (Poland), Czech (Bohemia) and Rus (Russia). Czech, despite all attempts to preserve it, has only a few leaves left on its ancient branches.

Rogalin chapel

Route 8

Through the little-known southeast

★★★ Warsaw – ★★ Kazimierz Dolny –★ Lublin – ★★ Zamosc – ★ Przemysl –★ Zakopane – ★★ High Tatra (786km/49 miles) *See map on pages 50–1*

This route is full of fascinating contrasts: unspoilt nature, solitude and wilderness alternate with the outstanding architecture of such places as Zamorsc and Lancut. In order to find a bed in this region it is essential to make reservations in advance: with the exception of the winter sports resort Zakopane, the southeast of Poland, formerly Galicia, has few tourist facilities. The tour is equally attractive in summer and winter and takes approximately 10 days. A car is the best means of transport since the infrastructure of the region is not yet very well developed, especially in the mountains.

Leaving Warsaw the city in the direction of Deblin, following the road along the east bank of the Vistula, you will be rewarded with a stretch of fine scenery along the river on your way to **Pulawy**. In the middle of this rather ugly industrial town is the romantic park of the Czartoryski family: the 'Gothic House' in this park is Poland's first public museum. Otherwise Pulawy has little to offer.

It is now only 14km (9 miles) to ★★ **Kazimierz Dolny** (pop. 5,000; 136km/85 miles). Described without exaggeration as one of the most beautiful places in Poland, the town has captivated generations of artists with its Mediterranean flair. The Old Town, with its picturesque Market Square, has probably been immortalised on canvas hundreds of times.

Kazimierz Dolny: scenes from the Market square

The attractive late Renaissance and Manneristic facades of the houses on the Market Square testify to the prosperity of the grain merchants who made the town what it is. The parish church above the Market Square is an example of the Lublin Renaissance style, characterised by the particularly elaborate stuccowork with which the vault is decorated. Dominating the town is the 14th-century ruin of the **Royal Castle**. Kazimierz the Great is said to have kept his Jewish lover Esterka here: a tunnel which connected the royal residence in town with the castle allowed the king to visit his lady love unseen.

Grain merchant's house facade

Royal ruins

★ **Lublin** (pop. 350,000; 187km/117 miles) could not be more of a contrast, either from the point of view of size or atmosphere. This otherwise provincial town is considerably enlivened by the presence of two universities, the Catholic and the State University of Lublin, and the population is also swelled by numerous travelling salesmen from the nearby states on Poland's eastern border.

The historic city centre is dominated by the ★ **castle**. The most important building in this complex is the Gothic Castle Chapel, its entire interior decorated with wall paintings in the Ruthenian/Byzantine style, which in the Gothic surroundings seem positively exotic. Today the primarily neo-Gothic complex houses a museum of Polish painting, folk art and archaeology. At the foot of the castle hill is the medieval city centre, and to the west are remains of the former city wall, dating from the 14th century, with the Cracow Gate (Brama Krakowska). Like many of the buildings in the Old Town, the cathedral is also a jumble of styles. The facade, rebuilt in 1819, is neoclassical, while the interior is a fine example of the baroque style. The neighbouring Dominican church – originally a Gothic building – has several interesting domed chapels in the late Renaissance style.

Axe of defiance

Zamosc – an architectural gem

The little Renaissance town of ★★ **Zamosc** (pop. 55,000; 272km/170 miles) is an architectural gem. In no other town in Poland or western Europe – with the exception of Italy, the home of the Renaissance – has this building style been so perfectly preserved. In 1580 the Polish chancellor Jan Zamoyski commissioned the Venetian architect Bernardo Morando to design a town in the middle of the countryside: the result was this classic example of European town architecture in the Renaissance period.

The ★ **Town Hall**, with its 50-m (165-ft) octagonal tower, crowned with a baroque helmet, dominates the Great Market Square. The double staircase was added to this late Renaissance building in the 18th century and reflects the theatricality of the baroque style. It blends in so well, however, that many visitors are astonished to learn that it was built much later. The square is lined with the most beautiful burghers' houses connected by arcaded passages. Southwest of the square, the Collegiate Church, richly decorated with sculptures and stuccowork, is a further example of Bernardo Morando's consummate artistry.

Zamosc can still be admired in all its former glory today because it was spared during the war. The Nazis in fact had plans of a quite different nature for it: the Polish citizens were to be expelled and the town was to become a 'German outpost' renamed 'Himmlerstadt' and repopulated with ethnic Germans. As we know, the course of events took another turn and Zamosc was saved.

The Old Town Square

The road to **Lancut** (pop. 16,000; 409km/256 miles) illustrates just how sparsely populated this southeastern part of Poland is. Lancut is the location of one of the most magnificent aristocratic residences in Poland; the early baroque ⋆ **palace** in the eastern part of the town was built in 1629–41 and has over 300 rooms. Today it is a museum of interior design. The **Carriage Museum** in the southern part of the extensive palace park is the largest collection of its kind in Europe with over 50 exhibits.

Part of the carriage collection

From Lancut proceed to ⋆ **Przemysl** (pop. 65,000; 476km/298 miles) on the River San. On top of the hill is the ⋆ **castle** built by Kazimierz the Great in the 14th century, but which was later reconstructed in the Renaissance style. Further down is the cathedral; the foundation stone for the original Gothic church was laid in 1460, and in 1724–44 this was rebuilt in the baroque style. The cathedral's foundations indicate that there was once an early Romanesque church on this site. In World War I the fortress of Przemysl played a key part in the confrontations between Russia and Austria-Hungary.

The village of **Krasiczyn**, 10km (6 miles) to the west, with its famous ⋆ **castle**, is worth a stop along the way. This impressive Renaissance building was commissioned by the Krasicki family in the year 1580; its most outstanding features are its four towers, all completely different, and the facade with its sgraffito decorations. It is surrounded by a splendid park.

Krasiczyn castle

Krasiczyn marks the start of the most beautiful stretch of this route, the road winding through magnificent mountain scenery with panoramic views of green valleys. Your first destination is **Sanok** (pop. 35,000; 548km/343 miles). This town is an ideal starting point for excursions in the Bieszczady, a range of mountains forming part of the Carpathians. There is an interesting collection of icons in the **Palace of Sanok** high up on the banks of the San and the open-air museum with examples of the architecture of the Lemks and Boyks, the two Ukrainian groups which lived in this area, is also well worth a visit.

Rafting on the Dunajec

Children of the Bieszczady

The boatmen wear their local costume

Lesko, only 13km (8 miles) from Sanok, marks the beginning (or end) of the Bieszczady loop road, a 160-km (99-mile) route through the beautiful scenery of the south-east tip of Poland. Those with hiking boots in their luggage will want to set out on foot, as there are some splendid trails through this unspoilt mountain region. If you have a tent and a little more time to spare, it is worth staying here for a few days to explore the countryside more thoroughly. In 1973 the outer edge of the Polish Carpathians was turned into ★ **Bieszczady National Park**. The highest peak, the Tarnica (1,346m/4,416ft), is located here and the unspoilt conifer and beech woods are still inhabited by wolves, lynxes and brown bears.

From Sanok, continue via Krosno and the attractive little town of Biecz to **Nowy Sacz** (pop. 73,000; 688km/430 miles). Although it has several buildings of architectural interest, including the parish church, Franciscan church and an open-air museum, most tourists come here in search of nature, en route to the ★ **Pieniny National Park** which is soon reached on the good road from Nowy Sacz. With an area of less than 3,000ha (7,413 acres), it is one of the smallest of the Polish national parks, but makes up for its lack of size in scenic beauty and its enormous variety of plant species. The high point of a visit to this park is a ★★ **raft trip** on the Dunajec. The long rafts (departing from the Katy quay at Sromowce) are steered by the local highlanders. Cutting through the Pieniny mountains near the Slovakian border the river forms a gorge almost 15km (9 miles) long between walls of rock 300m (984ft) high. The raft trip ends in Szczawnica.

Nowy Targ (pop. 28,000; 765km/478 miles) is an industrial centre with little to offer the tourist except on market day, which is every Thursday, when there is everything to be had from Tatra sheepdogs to horses and wooden toys to cowbells. From here, however, an excursion to **Debno** is a must. The church of ★★ **St Michael the Archangel** is one of the most important buildings in Poland. Unlike anything that has been seen up to now, this church is made entirely of larchwood panels joined with wooden pins: there is not one metal nail in the building. The interior is covered with beautiful late Gothic stencil painting.

Debno: carved figure of Christ

The wooden architecture in many of the small mountain villages of this region is the most striking example of the culture of the highlanders, a strong ethnic group in Poland whose traditions, including their dialect and costumes, are still very much part of their everyday life. That the highlanders were able to build so many fine houses is paradoxically due to the former poverty of this group, which drove large numbers out of the country to America. In accordance with tradition, the emigrés supported the relatives they had left behind. Today most highlanders make their money letting rooms to tourists, but some still earn their living as sheep farmers, producing two popular, traditional cheeses, *bryndza* and *oscypek*.

★ **Zakopane** (pop. 33,000) is the gateway to one of the greatest of Poland's natural treasures, the beautiful Tatra mountain chain and is a winter sports metropolis boasting good ski slopes, several ski jumps and over 50 ski lifts. What was once a highland village has now become a busy town. In many of the smaller places surrounding it, however, it is still possible to enjoy the peace and quiet of the mountains. The **Tatra Museum** in Zakopane includes exhibits relating to the customs of the highlanders and a natural history collection.

Souvenir beads in Zakopane

Zakopane once hosted the Winter Olympic Games, and is therefore well provided with tourist accommodation: there are a number of comfortable hotels, youth hostels, mountain huts and several hundred guesthouses.

The whole area of the ★★ **Tatra Mountains** has been turned into two national parks, one on the Polish side of the border and the other in Slovakia. With peaks of over 2,000m (6,500ft), this enchanting mountain range is the home of golden eagles, marmots, chamois and lynxes. With its alpine scenery and abundance of streams, waterfalls and lakes, there are numerous beautiful spots to visit and an assortment of trails covering everything from a gentle stroll to a climb. The paths are well marked and mountain climbing in the Tatras is greatly facilitated by the professional support of the local mountain guides. The famous mountain lake ★ **Morskie Oko** (literally sea eye) is the most popular beauty spot; splendidly located at a height of 1,400m (4,593ft), this 35-ha (86-acre) lake is easily accessible.

Hiking in the Tatras

Artists under the arches

Route 9

★★★ Cracow – the real capital of Poland?

Cracow candyfloss

The best way to visit Cracow (pop. 751,000) is to arrive early in the morning and go straight to the Old Town on foot, while it is still swathed in the rising morning mist. Every single stone of the 1,000-year-old city has a story to tell: of the dragon which fed on beautiful girls, or the tale of Wanda, who threw herself into the Vistula rather than marry her German suitor, or of Queen Jadwiga, who loved a German, but for reasons of state was forced to marry the wild heathen Jagiello. Before Jadwiga died of grief she gave her royal crown and entire fortune to the University of Cracow and had herself buried in a wooden coffin. The stones might also tell of a trumpeter who saved the city from an impending Mongol invasion and died in the process with an arrow in his throat, or of a grieving king, whose beloved wife died and was restored to life for a moment by a magician.

The sound of bells fills the morning air, pigeons coo and the first students mingle with the drunks of the previous night, the flower sellers set up their stalls and a restaurant where kings held banquets 700 years ago opens its doors. Perhaps it is true after all that this is the real capital of the country, where the crumbling plaster is genuine and not an imitation, where theatre and cabarets still attract enthusiastic audiences, and the contemplative lifestyle and sense of history among the people contrast sharply with the hectic pace of political, money-making Warsaw.

History

Two dates stand out in the city's history: the year 1000, when the diocese of Cracow was founded and the basis for the city's prosperity established, and the year 1364, when the Jagiellon University of Cracow was founded, the first in the country and the second in Central Europe after the University of Prague. From the 14th century, it was Poland's capital city when the Polish kings ruled from Cracow at Wawel Castle.

Although in the 17th century the city lost its political importance, it continued as the cultural capital of Poland. The tolerant imperial and royal monarchy allowed it to become the 'Polish Piemont', in an age when it was even forbidden to speak Polish in the schools of Warsaw.

In World War II, scheduled for destruction by the Nazis, by a stroke of good fortune Cracow was able to escape the fate of Warsaw and survived the war unharmed. A new threat, however, was already on the way. In the 1950s the huge steelworks Nowa Huta were built on the edge of the city, with the idea of introducing a 'proletarian element', represented by the 30,000 steelworkers, to counterbalance the old Cracow intellectual elite and impose the socialist spirit upon the royal city. As a result, Nowa Huta is having a disastrous effect on the priceless historical monuments of Cracow, which is compounded by the pollution from the industry of Upper Silesia, carried in this direction by the frequent west winds. The sulphurous fumes are eating away at the old buildings, and it is only thanks to the constant attentions of the restorers that the damage is not worse.

Sights

Cracow is a city full of historical monuments. The centre has remained largely unchanged since the Middle Ages when it was built. The city walls were left standing until the 19th century, when they were replaced by a green belt, the so-called Planty which today surrounds the entire city centre and marks the border of the no-traffic zone.

Souvenirs at the foot of Wawel Hill

On a walk round Cracow's ★★★ **Old Town** and up Wawel Hill, visiting the old buildings, the long history of the city gradually becomes palpably alive. Walk past the 15th-century ★ **Barbican** ❶, a circular defensive bastion in front of the gate, to enter the Old Town through ★ **Florian's Gate** (brama Florianska). It is the only gate in the old remaining pieces of the city wall to have been preserved. The gate and the adjoining sections of wall with their fortified towers date from the 13th and 14th centuries. Today artists use the walls as an open-air gallery for their work, with everything on offer from views of the city in every imaginable style to weeping gypsy ladies. Follow the wall to **Czartoryski Palace** ❷, which houses a fine collection of Italian, German and Dutch masters, including the world-famous painting *Lady with Ermine* by Leonardo da Vinci.

Florian's Gate

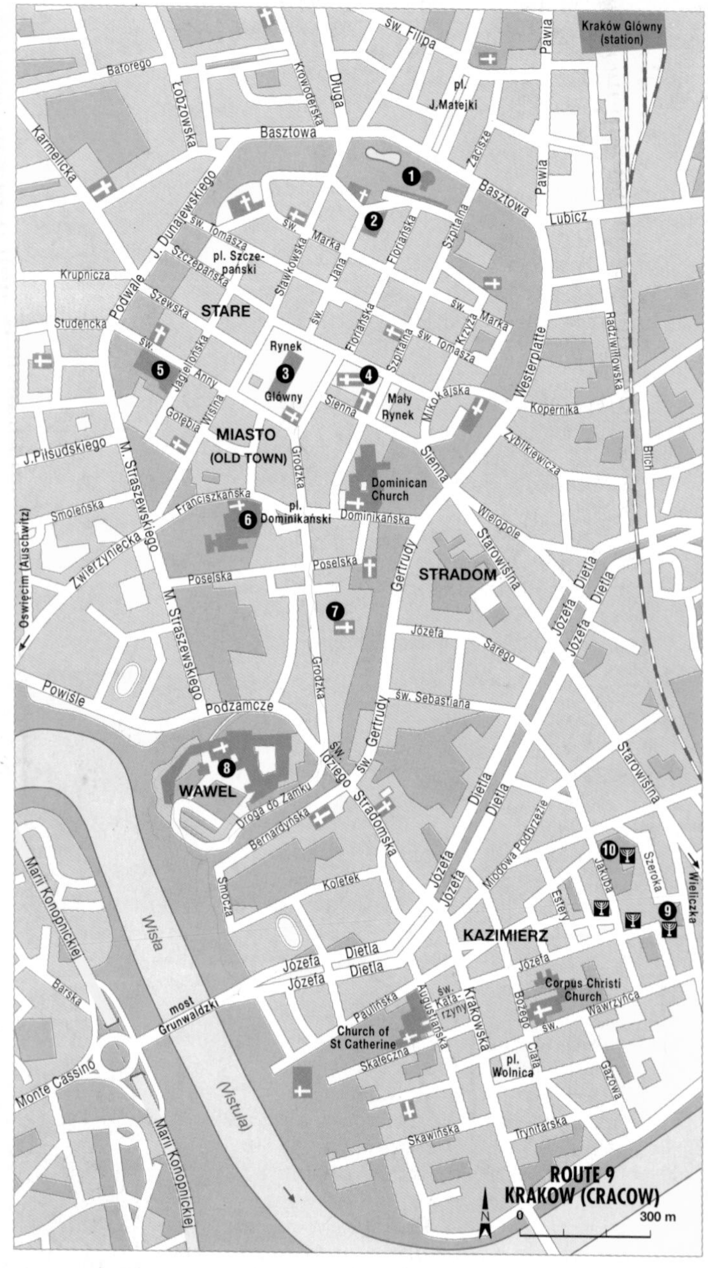
Kraków Główny (station)
św. Filipa
Pawia
Batorego
Łobzowska
Krowoderska
Długa
pl. J.Matejki
Basztowa
Karmelicka
Zacisze
Basztowa
Pawia
Lubicz
J. Dunajewskiego
św. Tomasza
Szczepańska
pl. Szczepański
Sławkowska
św. Marka
Floriańska
Szpitalna
Jana
Krupnicza
Podwale
Szewska
STARE
Studencka
św. Marka
św. Krzyża
Westerplatte
Radziwiłłowska
św. Anny
Jagiellońska
Rynek
Główny
św. Tomasza
Floriańska
Szpitalna
Sienna
Mały Rynek
Mikołajska
Kopernika
Gołębia
Wiślna
MIASTO
(OLD TOWN)
J.Piłsudskiego
M. Straszewskiego
Grodzka
Sienna
Zyblikiewicza
Dominican Church
Franciszkańska
pl. Dominikański
Dominikańska
Smoleńska
Zwierzyniecka
Oświęcim (Auschwitz)
Wielopole
Starowiślna
Poselska
Poselska
Gertrudy
STRADOM
Dietla
Dietla
Józefa
Józefa
M. Straszewskiego
Józefa
Sarego
Grodzka
Powiśle
Podzamcze
św. Sebastiana
św. Idziego
św. Gertrudy
Starowiślna
WAWEL
Droga do Zamku
Bernardyńska
Stradomska
Dietla
Dietla
Podbrzezie
Miodowa
Józefa
Józefa
Szeroka
Wieliczka
Jakuba
Estery
Marii Konopnickiej
Wisła
Smocza
Koletek
KAZIMIERZ
Dietla
Dietla
Józefa
Józefa
Józefa
Corpus Christi Church
Barska
most Grunwaldzki
Paulińska
Augustiańska
św. Katarzyny
Krakowska
Bożego
św. Wawrzyńca
Ciała
Church of St Catherine
Skałeczna
pl. Wolnica
Gazowa
Monte Cassino
Marii Konopnickiej
(Vistula)
Skawińska
Trynitarska
ROUTE 9
KRAKOW (CRACOW)
N
0
300 m

Florian's Street (ulica Florianska), leading into the centre of the Old Town from the gate, is a popular place to stroll. Before following the stream of tourists and residents to the Market Square, however, pay a visit to the traditional artists' café Jama Michalikowa at No. 45 and enjoy a coffee with milk in the homely atmosphere provided by the Viennese Secession-style surrounings. Even in Vienna itself it would be hard to find its equal.

Fortified by this refreshment, continue now on to the huge ★★ **Cracow Market Square** (Rynek Glowny) in the heart of Cracow. Of all the medieval market squares in Europe only St Mark's Square in Venice is larger. The Cracow flower sellers spread out their colourful wares, parents buy their children candy floss or the typical pastry rings sold from glass carts, people occupy the surrounding cafés, which put their tables outside with the first rays of sun, or stand around in small groups discussing the day's news. The building that dominates the square is the ★ **Cloth Hall** ❸ (Sukiennice), which still fulfils its original function as a trading centre. The complex actually dates from the 14th century, but was so beautifully rebuilt during the Renaissance era that it became a source of inspiration to many architects elsewhere. The most frequently copied aspect was the attic, which conceals a steep roof, with the retaining wall richly ornamented with masked heads.

Souvenir dolls

The Rynek Glowny is lined with patricians' houses from all epochs. The east side of the square is taken up by the imposing **St Mary's Church** ❹. A 14th-century basilica with three aisles, its two towers of differing design are its dominant features. Every hour to the present day, the famous trumpet fanfare which warned the sleeping city of the impending Mongol invasion in the 13th century, is played live from the left-hand tower.

St Mary's church

The famous ★★ **main altar** of St Mary's is a masterpiece of late Gothic carving. Veit Stoss of Nuremberg (or Wit Stwosz, as he was known to the Poles), who was summoned to Cracow for this purpose, worked on the winged altarpiece from 1477 to 1489. Standing 13 metres (43ft) high, it is the largest medieval altar in existence. Stoss was held in high esteem in the then Polish capital, which also had an influential German aristocratic community, and he remained here for almost 20 years, completing several works for the Polish nobility and the Jagiellon king. Every day at noon the altar is ceremoniously opened (and remains open until 6pm), revealing the full extent of Stoss's genius in the central panel, an impressive representation of the death of the Virgin Mary.

Collegium Maius

From the market proceed to the oldest remaining building of Cracow University, the ★ **Collegium Maius** ❺. Lectures and graduation ceremonies are still held here, where there is a beautiful Gothic arcaded courtyard. In the University Museum (only open in the mornings) are memorabilia of the institution's most famous students, including the astronomer Nicholas Copernicus.

Return to the market and follow the ulica Grodzka in the direction of Wawel Castle to the ★ **Franciscan Church** ❻ with its rather bold combination of styles. The Gothic interior is decorated with brightly coloured Art Nouveau windows by the Polish turn-of-the-century genius, Stanislaw Wyspianski, who was an artist and dramatist and belonged to a movement called Young Poland which brought painting and poetry together through theatre. Continuing on to Wawel Hill, take a look at the ★ **Church of St Peter and St Paul** ❼, the first baroque church in Poland. The architect modelled this church, built for the Jesuits, on the famous Jesuit church, Il Gesù, in Rome.

Wawel Hill ❽

The fine collection of buildings of ★★★ **Wawel Hill** blend together in a variety of styles to form a remarkably harmonic complex. The **Cathedral** is important not only as a religious building, but also for the part it has played in the nation's history. For centuries, beginning in 1320, this was the place where Polish kings were crowned and they are buried in the crypt together with religious leaders and national heroes, who in Poland include poets (Adam Mickiewicz, *see page* 77) and painters. Inside the church are numerous side chapels, including the **Holy Cross Chapel** (Kaplica Swietokrzyska) with Ruthenian/Byzantinian frescoes and the marble sarcophagus of the Jagiellon king Kazimierz IV, another work by Veit Stoss. The most impressive chapel is without a doubt the **Sigismund Chapel** (Kaplica Zygmuntowska) with its dome of pure gold.

The Cathedral entrance: bones of contention

The **Royal Castle** is as magnificent as befits a building that was the residence of the Polish rulers for generations, and it is embellished inside and out with impressive works of art from different centuries. The present exterior dates back to 1502–1536 when the palace was rebuilt in the Renaissance style. The courtyard, surrounded by arcades, also dates back to this period: elegant and harmonically proportioned, it is one of the most outstanding examples of its kind in Europe. It was painted by Hans Dürer, the less famous brother of the great Albrecht Dürer.

Dragon statue

The **State Art Collections** cover an astonishing range of exhibits: gold swords, royal insignias, jewellery and military equipment, including ancient cut-and-thrust weapons, as well as clocks, furniture and pottery. The most valuable items are the 136 tapestries which the last Jagiellon king, Zygmunt II Augustus, had made in Flanders.

Kazimierz

Flea market in Kazimierz

Historically an independent city with its own town hall, market place and churches, Kazimierz was founded in the 14th century, just south of the old city borders, by Kazimierz the Great in an attempt to undermine the economic supremacy of the proud aristocratic town of Cracow. From 1495 a large Jewish population grew up here and Kazimierz became known as Cracow's Jewish Quarter with laws of its own. The Jews lived there until 1941 when the Nazis cleared them out by first sending them to a ghetto and then on to the gas chambers.

The Jewish cemetery

The Jewish Museum in the former ★ **Old Synagogue** ❾ (Stara Synagogy) is a reminder of the great Jewish culture that once flourished here. The nearby **Jewish Cemetery** ❿, also called the Remu'h Cemetery after a famous rabbi, was laid out in 1533, and is one of only two remaining Renaissance Jewish cemeteries in Europe (the other is in Prague). The Jewish buildings of Kazimierz escaped destruction by the Nazis, who intended to set up a museum of 'vanished races' – as it was officially called – here. Of the 68,000 Jewish inhabitants of Kazimierz in 1938, only a few hundred survived the extermination camps: that these individuals were saved was due in no small part to the efforts of German trader Oskar Schindler, whose part in the war was movingly portrayed in Steven Spielberg's epic movie *Schindler's List*.

The Madonna carved from salt

Wieliczka salt mines

Take the suburban railway or bus to Wieliczka 20 km (13 miles) outside Cracow to Poland's oldest ★★ **working salt mines**. Their fantastic salt sculptures and the underground cathedral carved out of salt have been attracting visitors from all over the world for 250 years. Over 300,000 people now come each year to visit the complex, which is

Monument to miners

on UNESCO's World Cultural Heritage list, taking the lifts hundreds of feet down below the surface. Salt was already being mined in Wieliczka in the 12th century, and possibly even before the year 1000, making these without a doubt the oldest salt mines in the world. The deposits, which are mined at eight levels, go down to a depth of 315m (1,034ft) and the total length of all the galleries, chambers, and tunnels is over 150km (93 miles).

Auschwitz (Oswiecim)

Situated over 50km (32 miles) west of Cracow, the town itself is of no particular interest as no one anywhere in the world would associate the name Auschwitz with an industrial town between Cracow and Upper Silesia. Instead Auschwitz will remain a synonym for the most horrific genocide in history. The memorial in the grounds of the Auschwitz concentration camp – where in 1995 the 50th anniversary of its liberation by the Russians was celebrated – and the second memorial in Birkenau (Brzezinka), the camp 4km (2½ miles) to the west, commemorate the 1.5 million people who died here as victims of Nazi racist fanaticism.

Cardinal at Auschwitz

Established in April 1940, 'Auschwitz I' was reserved for political prisoners, mainly Poles and Germans, as well as Soviet prisoners of war. More than 100,000 people lost their lives here. But it was in Birkenau, or 'Auschwitz II', established in 1941, that the SS developed their huge extermination complex, where over a million people of Jewish origin were gassed. Guides provide objective background information on the site, but nothing can diminish the horror of this industrial extermination factory, with its 'bathhouses', corpse cellars and cremating ovens. Children under 13 are not admitted.

The main gate

Route 10

Silesian contrasts

★★★ Cracow – Czestochowa – Opole –★★ Wroclaw – Karkonoscze Mountains (511km/319 miles) *See maps on pages 50–1 and 72*

The highlight of this route to the border of eastern Germany is the old Silesian metropolis of Wroclaw. The scenic beauty of Silesia, old spas and hiking trails through the Sudety Mountains as well as major art treasures are among the attractions which await you. Unfortunately, though, you will not fail to notice the the environmental damage that is being inflicted on this part of the country.

The Catholicism of Poland can be experienced in one of the most popular places of pilgrimage in the world: Czestochowa, where religious tourism is exploited to the full. Those who want to enjoy the countryside as well as absorb the culture should allow at least six days for this route. To climb the Sniezka or go for a longer hike in the Sudety requires a few days more. There are newly opened guesthouses at all the places on this route, so finding a room should not be a problem.

Pilgrims in Czestochowa

After the concentrated culture of Cracow the ★ **Ojcow National Park** only a few kilometres north of the city is a welcome contrast. It is a typical erosion landscape of extraordinary beauty, with flat limestone hills, deeply carved valleys and bizarre stone and cliff formations shaped like clubs, needles, towers and gates. The symbol of the park, in fact, is the famous Hercules' Club, an unusual pillar of rock by the side of the road. At the northern end of the park is Pieskowa Skala, which has a beautiful early ★ **Renaissance castle** with an elegant arcaded courtyard, museum and adjoining restaurant.

By the time you enter Upper Silesia, if not before, you will be thinking back longingly to the tranquillity of the Ojcow National Park, especially when the Huta Katowice (near Dabrowa Gornicza) comes into view. Today no one knows what to do with this huge factory built during the 'Gierek epoch' (1970–80) with huge loans from the West.

Czestochowa Basilica

Czestochowa (pop. 250,000; 126km/79 miles) offers a complete contrast of a different kind – one of the most popular places of pilgrimage for Roman Catholics in the world. However, an opportunity for quiet contemplation is not necessarily what you will find. The object of the millions of devout pilgrims, who come every year to the baroque monastery of Jasna Gora, is the ★★ **Black Madonna**, a small Byzantine icon of unknown age. Like

Pilgrims arrive in the town

the Black Madonnas of Monserrat, Altötting and Guadalupe, the Czestochowa Madonna is steeped in legend.

The picture is an example of a particular style of Byzantine icon painting where dark colours were used. In no other country in the world has a single work of art had such religious, social and above all political significance as Poland's **Black Madonna**. In the first Swedish war in 1655, the **Black Madonna** strengthened the resistance of the Polish patriots, and the Swedes failed to take Czestochowa. This rather unimportant military victory had a symbolic effect, and as a result the Poles were able to drive the Swedes right out of the country. King Kasimierz ceremoniously laid down his crown before the Madonna and in 1717 she was officially declared 'Queen of Poland'.

The icon, donated in 1384 by Duke Wladyslaw of Opole, is of no particular artistic significance, but it is still Poland's greatest national relic. The monastery itself was founded by the Pauline order; it was built on a hill to the west of the original town centre in 1382 and fortified in the 17th century. Today the complex is dominated by the Gothic ★ **monastery church**, dating from 1463, and is surrounded by bastions and monastery buildings.

Queueing to see the Black Madonna

The **Black Madonna** is located over a priceless early baroque altar made of ebony and silver. Normally the picture is covered by a cloth, but it is unveiled with great ceremony every day before the first mass and is covered up again at midday. Crowds of pilgrims and tourists press round the holy picture, which almost makes you forget to visit the treasury with its valuable relics and the impressive Knights' Hall of the baroque monastery.

The route continues to **Opole** (pop. 120,000; 224km/140 miles). Originally the site of a fort constructed by the Opole tribe, the town itself, situated on the right bank of the River

Odra, was founded in 1217. There are many reminders of its early history, including the massive tower of the Piast Castle.

The Market Square is dominated by a town hall, which seems to belong in Italy rather than in Poland. This is no coincidence, since it is in fact a copy of the Palazzo Veccio in Florence. The sacred buildings of Opole, however, are the genuine article: the cathedral by the Odra really is Gothic, and dates back to the 15th century. The Franciscan monastery and its church also date from the mid-14th century. Both churches contain tombs of Piast princes of Opole. Don't leave without a visit to the **Opole Village Museum** outside the town, an open-air museum featuring historic wooden peasant houses from the region (Tuesday to Sunday 10am–5pm).

Brzeg (pop. 37,000; 267km/167 miles) boasts a magnificent ★ **castle**, arranged round a courtyard with arcades on several floors. Built by the Slavic princes of the Piast dynasty, it is one of the most important Renaissance monuments in Poland and was probably modelled on Wawel Castle in Cracow.

★★ **Wroclaw** (pop. 643,600; 309km/193 miles) owes its development to its ideal position on the Odra in the centre of the Silesian lowlands on the road linking Western Europe with Russia. The city dates back to the 10th century when a settlement was established on the Ostrow Tumski. Later the Slezanie built a castle here, and in the year 1000, the king of Poland founded the first diocese on Polish soil here.

Wroclaw resident

Wroclaw has changed nationality several times in the course of its history. When Silesia was still the most important province in the former Polish Piast state, Wroclaw was the centre of the region. In 1335 it came under Bohemian rule, belonged to the Habsburgs from 1526 and was captured by the Prussians in 1741. Finally, this century, it went back to being a Polish city after years as part of the German Reich under the name of Breslau. After the flight or expulsion of the German population, Wroclaw was primarily resettled by Polish exiles from the present-day Ukraine.

Town Hall Beer cellar and detail of planetary clock

The interesting places to visit are all clustered round the centre within walking distance of one another. Most of the historic buildings destroyed in the war have been reconstructed. The ★★ **Town Hall** ❶ is considered to be one of the finest Gothic secular buildings in Central Europe, featuring an artistic facade richly decorated with tracery. Its rooms, also back to their original condition with fine inlaid panelling, Renaissance painting and magnificent vaulting, are open to the public. The beer cellar dates from the 15th century.

Church of St Mary Magdalene

Not far from the Town Hall is the red brick building of **St Mary Magdalene's Church** ❷, dating from the 14th century, featuring a 12th-century Romanesque portal from a nearby abbey incorporated in its outer wall. The tower of the Gothic church, **St Elizabeth's** ❸, is the highest in the city, but the church has not yet been restored after fire damage in 1974. North of the old town, by the Odra, are the buildings of the ★ **University of Wroclaw** ❹. In the Collegium Maximum, the main building which was constructed in 1728–41, is the **Aula Leopoldina**, without a doubt the most beautiful baroque hall in Poland, where architecture, frescoes and sculpture blend together to form a perfect work of art.

Cross the bridge over the Odra to Piasek (sand) Island, which is dominated by the Gothic ★ **Church of St Mary on the Sand** ❺ (Kosciol Sw Panny na Piasku). The most distinguishing features of the interior are several late-Gothic altars and the modern windows. A small bridge leads across to the Ostrow Tumski, (Cathedral Island), which is not really an island any more now that one arm of the Odra has been filled in. This was the original centre of Wroclaw under the Slavic princes. The first church you come to is not the cathedral itself but the **Holy Cross Church** ❻ (Kosciol Sw Krzyza), an elegant Gothic build-

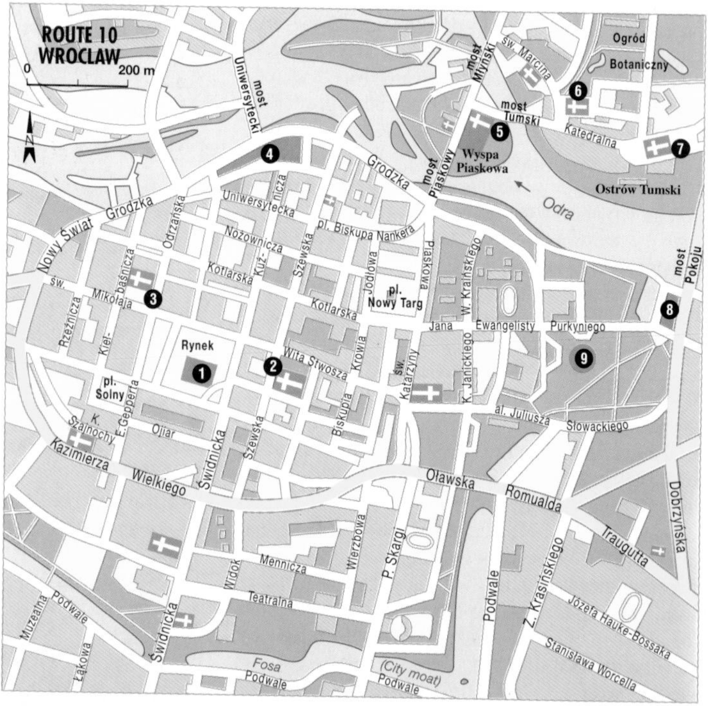

In the Kawiarnia Café

ing which rather unusually incorporates two churches. On the lower 'floor', which resembles a large crypt, is the Greek-Catholic (Uniate) Church of St Bartholomew's, and above it the Holy Cross Church.

Walk past the 18th-century archbishop's residence to the ★ **cathedral** ❼ (Katedra Sw Jana Chrzciciela). This massive church, begun in the 13th century, dominates its surroundings and is the most important building on the island. The special features of the interior are the three chapels of the ambulatory: St Elizabeth's to the south, an example of Italian high baroque, the Gothic Marian chapel and the oval Elector's Chapel, an example of Hapsburg baroque by the famous Fischer of Erlach. The ★ **National Museum** ❽ (Muzeum Narodwe) covers the full range of Silesian art, and has an important collection of Gothic wooden sculptures.

Ready for the road

After all these important architectural monuments, the next building you come to is a more recent, rather ordinary circular construction, but it is this that really draws the visitors. It houses the **Raclawice Panorama** ❾, a view of a battle on an impressive scale with a length of 150m (492ft) and a height of 15m (49ft). Paintings of this kind, which were hung in a round building to make them appear three-dimensional, were very popular in the last century until they were supplanted by the cinema. *The Raclawice Panorama*, painted in Lwow in 1893, depicts the victorious battle against the Russians in 1794.

After Wroclaw the route now leads south through the flat countryside to ★ **Swidnica** (pop. 60,000; 360km/225 miles) which has an immense building that catches your eye even if you are not particular interested in architecture: the Protestant ★ **Church of Peace**; today the Holy Trinity Church (Kosciol Sw Trojcy). Its most impressive aspect is the contrast between the rather ordinary half-timbering of the exterior and the magnificent interior. The devoutly Catholic Hapsburg monarchy decreed that only wood,clay, sand and straw should be used to build Protestant churches. The altar, pulpit and organ gleam with gold and the painting on the wooden ceiling adds to the splendour. The huge building holds 7,500 worshippers.

It is impossible to ignore the effects of industrial pollution in Poland, and **Walbrzych** (pop.140,000; 383km/239 miles) is no exception with its surroundings dominated by massive slag heaps and steelworks. Although this industrial town is itself not very attractive, there are several places of interest in its vicinity. The most rewarding of these is ★ **Ksiaz Castle**, the largest castle in Silesia. It was erected in the mid-16th century on the site of an older complex, dating from the 13th century, and was rebuilt in the 19th century. Unfortunately, the castle and the surrounding rhododendron park is badly in need of renovation.

Refreshments at Krzeszow

Another major tourist attraction about 20km (12 miles) away from Walbrzych, is ★★ **Krzeszow Monastery**, the most important late baroque monastery in Silesia. Founded by Benedictine monks in the 13th century, it was taken over by the Cistercians only a short time afterwards. It is dominated by the richly decorated facade of the Church of the Assumption with its twin towers which, if not the work of Kilian Ignaz Dientzenhofer, as has been thought, must be that of an equally gifted architect.

Views of Jelenia Gora

Like Krzeszow, **Jelenia Gora** (pop. 95,000; 445km/278 miles) is in the Sudety Mountains. Set in a valley ringed by mountains, it is a good starting point for excursions into the attractive countryside and is full of tourists during the summer. Whitewashed houses with ground-floor arcades line the fine Market Square; together with the town hall, which was built at a later date in the 18th century, and is the focal point of the Old Town.

The main tourist centre is the old spa **Cieplice Slaskie Zdroj** with its hot sulphur springs, which is now a suburb of Jelenia Gora. Records show that in 1281 the Knights of St John were already making use of the healing properties of the springs to cure skin diseases, so that Cieplice can genuinely claim to be one of the oldest spas in the world. It had its heyday in the 18th and 19th centuries, when it was a gathering place of the rich and beautiful rather than patients in search of a cure.

It is not clear from his writings to which group the German poet Goethe belonged, all that we know is that he too went on excursions to the **Sniezka** (1,602m/5,255ft), the highest peak in the Karkonosze Mountains; this ridge that forms part of the Sudety is still a popular hiking and recreation area.

The most beautiful parts of the ★★ **Karkonosze Mountains** including the Sniezka have been turned into a **national park** covering an area of 56sq km (22sq miles). It is divided by the Polish/Czech border, the Polish part being smaller but no less interesting than the Czech part. Getting to the top of the Sniezka is no problem, especially since part of the ascent can be made in a chairlift. Once wooded, the summit was stripped of its trees generations ago, and attempts at reforestation have been unsuccessful.

Crafts of the Karkonosze

At the foot of the Sniezka is **Karpacz**. One of the first tourist resorts, it was created in 1960 by combining the former village of Krummhubel with several other nearby villages and hamlets, and spreads uphill with a total height difference of 400m (1,312ft) between the various districts.

Lazarus carving at Wang

The district of Bierutowice has an architectural curiosity that is unexpected in this part of the world: the wooden ★ **Wang Chapel** from the village of Wang in southern Norway. In the 19th century the community was obliged to sell the 13th-century church, which had become too small for the congregation; it was dismantled and eventually arrived by a roundabout route at Bierutowice where it was painstakingly reassembled. Although it is rather unlikely that, as is maintained, the two dragon's heads projecting from the gable originally adorned the prows of Viking ships, their decorative effect is not in dispute. Many of the beams are decorated with mysterious carvings – including winged dragons and double faces.

Allow enough time for the last few kilometres through the park, since you will soon leave the mountains behind as you drive to the German border.

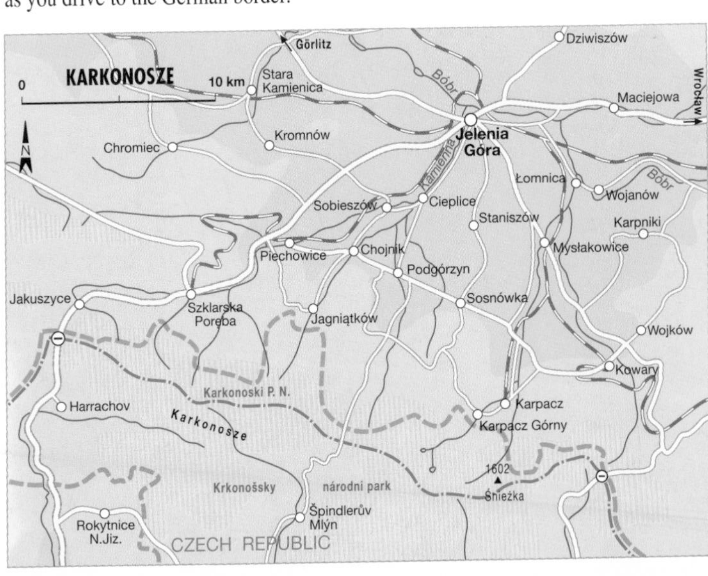

ADAM
MICKIEWICZ

The Arts

Opposite: Adam Mickiewicz

For decades Poland was proud of being the country that spent the highest amount of money per head on culture. This golden age however came to an end with the Communist era and now all areas of Polish culture, film, theatre, fine arts, music and literature are exposed to the cold wind of a disorganised market economy.

However, this has by no means dealt the death blow to Poland's cultural life, which is keeping up a highly respected international profile: the guest performances of Polish theatre groups are as enthusiastically applauded as ever, Polish musicians are a permanent fixture at many festivals and the high reputation of the Polish film industry still stands. This is due without a doubt to the deep-seated cultural awareness of the population, the long tradition of Polish culture and its place in the Polish concept of nationhood.

Events in Cracow

Literature

The greatest Polish Romantic poet, Adam Mickiewicz (1798–1855), extolled the freedom fighters and his epic poem *Pan Tadeusz* (1834) is an idealised picture of the Polish state. Due to foreign rule, like many other Poles active on the cultural scene, Mickiewicz lived in Paris. The decimated cultural elite of Poland was under similar pressure during the Communist era and many saw their only chance of artistic freedom in emigration. Some of the most famous and internationally known Poles on the cultural scene have lived abroad, such as writers Witold Gombrowicz, Stanislaw Mrozek, Czeslaw Milosz, Stanislaw Lem and Leszek Kolakowski. Their influential, usually determinedly anti-Communist opinions were nevertheless always heard in Communist Poland; many books were printed for a so-called 'second circulation' illegally, and were thus free from interference by the censors.

Bust of poet Michel Lengowski

Art

Since the Napoleonic wars, Polish art has had more in common with the West than with the East. As might be expected of a nation divided against its will, Polish art has dwelt in a world of hope and dreams rather than in one of political and economic realities, so it is probably safe to say that romanticism is at the heart of the country's art, particularly from 1830 to1918.

The fine arts had a slightly easier time with the Communists than literature. The Polish Poster School flourished from the 1960s, and its main representatives – Jan Lenica, Franciszek Starowieyski, Waldemar Swierzy – transformed the poster from an object designed for a specific purpose to an art form.

Chopin statue

Music

The development of Polish music grew on patriotic foundations. At a time when the concept of 'national music' was still unknown anywhere else, Chopin (*see below*)was already using elements of folk music in his works.

The modern music of Poland has also acquired an international reputation. Witold Lutoslwski and Krzysztof Penderecki, whose works may be difficult to listen to for those without experience of this type of music, rank as top composers. In 1992 music critics discovered the third symphony of a Katowice composer, Henryk Mikolaj Gorecki, written 17 years previously, which immediately became popular. Polish Jazz (Adam Makowicz, Michal Urbaniak) has made its name internationally, too.

Frederic Chopin (1810–49)

Chopin was born just outside Warsaw to a French father and Polish mother. He spent his youth in the capital and got to know all the folk songs and dances of the surrounding villages, which he used later in almost all his works. He made his piano-playing debut when he was still a young boy, playing in the elegant salons of the aristocracy and made his first attempts at composition, mainly polonaises, as a child.

In the autumn of 1830, Chopin left Warsaw, not knowing that he would never return. When in 1831, he heard that the Russians had moved in, he settled in Paris where he found world fame.

In 1836 he met the novelist George Sand – a complicated lover but also a caring friend – who looked after him during his long years of his ill health. He travelled with her to Majorca, where he composed his famous *Preludes,* the splendid *Polonaise in A major* and the *Second Sonata in B minor* which includes the funeral march. But his health continued to deteriorate. He returned to France and composed the *Polonaise in A flat major*. In 1847, George Sand left him. Lonely, ill and with little money, he fled to London, where he gave his last performance in public. He then returned to Paris, and died of tuberculosis in 1849.

Production of Merlin

Theatre and Cinema

Polish theatre ranges from the classic national repertoire (Mickiewicz, Slowacki, Wyspianski) to modern avant-garde theatre, influenced in the main by Jerzy Grotowski and his Poor Theatre (Teatr Ubogi) in Wroclaw and Tadeusz Kantor of Cracow.

The Polish film industry had plenty of financial support from the Communists for propaganda use, but there were still many who succeeded in establishing a style of their own and indirectly criticising the society. Others, such as Roman Polanski, saw emigration as the only solution.

Festivals

April *Poznan:* Springtime Music.

May *Cracow:* International Festival of Short-Feature Films.
Czestochowa: Festival of Sacral Music, 'Gaude Mater'.
Torun: International Theatrical Festival.
Wroclaw: Festival of Jazz Music 'Jazz on the Odra' (Jazz nad Odra).

June *Cracow:* Cracow Days (Dni Krakowa).
Kazimierz Dolny: Polish Folk Art Fair.
Posnan: International Theatrical Festival.
Stary Sacz: Festival of Old Music.

June–July *Warsaw:* Mozart Festival by the Warsaw Chamber Opera.

June–August *Gdansk:* International Festival of Organ, Choir and Chamber music. 'Musica Sacra'.

July *Jarocin (south of Poznan):* Rock Festival.
Zakopane: Karol Szymanowski Music Days.

August *Cracow:* 'Music in Old Cracow' Festival.
Duszniki-Zdroj (Lower Silesia): Chopin Festival in the open air.
Zakopane: International Festival of Highland Folklore.
Zielona Gora: International Festival of Folk Ensembles.

September 'Jazz Jamboree' international festival of jazz music.
Warsaw: International Festival of Contemporary Music 'Warsaw Autumn' (Warszawski jesien).
Wroclaw: International Oratorio and Cantata Festival 'Wratislavia Cantans'.

October *Warsaw:* Chopin International Piano Competition (every five years, next in 2000).
Warsaw Film Festival of foreign films.
Wroclaw: International Meetings of Open Theatre.

December *Wroclaw:* The 'Wro-Sound Basis Visual Art' international festival.

Cracow musician

Food and Drink

Polish meals are typically solid and traditional with a meat basis. Bread and vegetables, in particular potatoes, are also important elements in Polish cuisine, which has few regional differences. The most important national dish is *bigos*, a stew which includes sauerkraut, cabbage, wild mushrooms and meat. There are as many different recipes for it as there are housewives and cooks in Poland.

Barzcz (beetroot soup) and *zurek* (rye flour soup) are also popular. In summer try *chlodnik*, a delicious cold soup made of sour milk, beetroot, cucumber, ham and egg, rather like *barszcz*. Opinions are divided over *flaki* (tripe soup), but everyone likes the delicious *pierogi* which are square little pockets of dough stuffed with every imaginable filling: cheese, fruit, mushrooms or cabbage to name but a few. The juicy pork or beef pot roasts are turned into gourmet dishes with the addition of the tasty wild mushrooms found in the woods in Poland.

The Poles are very hospitable and economic crises and food shortages seem to be forgotten when there is a guest for a meal. The table will almost groan under the weight of the wide variety of dishes: 'When a guest is in the home, God is in the home' is an old Polish saying. Thus the guest is king not only in restaurants but in the simplest homes.

The most important drink is still vodka (wodka in Polish), which simply means 'little water'. As is well known, the Poles are the biggest producers and consumers of vodka in the world. The annual consumption of almost 12 litres (21 pints) a year of pure alcohol per head consists almost entirely of vodka. The statistics do not, however, take home-made spirits into account.

Since the recent restructuring of the Polish spirits monopoly Polmos, Polish vodka connoisseurs have been rather confused by the appearance of a host of new names alongside the traditional brands such as Zytnia, Wyborowa and Zubrowa: every distillery can now sell its own products at its own expense. However, far worse than the confusing choice of brands is the massive rise in the price of the 'water of life'. The price may perhaps achieve what all the prohibitions and restrictions of previous governments failed to do, namely bring down the high level of vodka consumption in the country, which is one of Poland's biggest social problems.

In every luxury class hotel you'll find a well-managed restaurant. In addition to national specialities, hotel kitchens offer a variety of simple, Middle European dishes. In large cities there are new restaurants opening up all the time.

Opposite: thirst quencher for a coachman

Organic vegetables in Cracow

Vodka: the national firewater

Tucking in at MacDonalds

Restaurant selection

Here are some restaurant suggestions for Poland's most popular destinations, comprising three categories: **$$$** (expensive); **$$** (moderate); **$** (cheap):

The elegant Wilanow in Warsaw

Warsaw

$$$U Fukiera, Rynek Starego miasta 27, tel: 311013. One of the most popular restaurants in Warsaw, excellent Polish cuisine. **$$$Belwedere**, Stara Pomaranczarnia, Lazienki, tel: 414806. An elegant restaurant in an attractive setting in Lazienki Park. **$$$Wilanow**, ul. Wiertnicza 27, in Wilanow, tel: 421852. Polish and international cuisine in a stylish atmosphere; specialises in venison. **$$Bazyliszek**, Rynek Starego Miasta 5/7, tel: 311841. In addition to a splendid view of the Old Town Square, the restaurant also has very good Polish cuisine. **$$Swietoszek**, ul. Jezuicke 6/8, tel: 315634. French cooking in the Old Town.

Beer pump in Gdansk

Cracow

$$$ Wierzynek, Rynek Glowny 15,tel:229896. The most famous restaurant in Poland: in this house, in 1346, a banquet was held for six emperors and kings plus numerous dukes and princes. The prices are equally exalted. **$$Hawelka**, Rynek Glowny 34, and **$$Staropolska**, ul. Sienna 4, tel:225821. Both offer good traditional Polish cuisine.

Gdansk

$$$Pod Lososiem, ul. Szeroka 51/54, tel: 317652. The most stylish restaurant in town, reservation essential. **$$Tawerna**, ul. Powroznicza 19/20. Traditional Polish cooking in the Old Town.

Café in Kolobrzeg

Szczecin

$$$Chief, ul. K. Swierczewskie 16, tel: 43765. The best place to go for seafood.

Swinoujscie

$$Albatros, ul. Powstancow Slaskich 1, tel: 0936-2335 and **$$Gryfia**, ul. Bohaterw Stalingradu 8; neither are gourmet restaurants but offer good, solid food.

Kolobrzeg

$$Fregata, ul. Dworcowa 12, the best restaurant in town; the hotel restaurants are also good.

Slupsk

$**Karczma Slupska**, ul. Wojska Polskiego 11; **Karczma pod Kluka**, ul. Kaszubska 22; both unpretentious restaurants with good traditional cuisine.

Leba
$Mewa, ul. Kosciuszki 50; **$Karczma Slowinska**, ul. Kosciuszki 28. Both have good, inexpensive food.

Malbork
$$$Zamkowa, Ul. Staroscinska 14, tel: 055-2736. Good Polish cooking.

Olsztyn
$$$Francuska, ul. Misckiewicza, tel: 089-275301. A tastefully furnished luxury restaurant with French cuisine; famous for its tender Chateaubriands but notorious for its high prices.

Gizycko
$$Grota, ul. Sienkiewicza 3. Located in a former East Prussian guard-house dating from 1864. **$$Mazurska**, ul. Warszawska 6, tel: 0887-862139. A restaurant with a folksy atmosphere.

Mikolajki
$Krol Sielaw, ul. Kajki 5, tel: 0887-16323. Good cuisine and friendly service.

Torun
$Staropolska, Zeglarska 10/14, tel: 056-26061. Good Polish cuisine, in the same building as the Staropolska Hotel. **$Staromiejska**, ul. Szczytna 2/4. Italian cooking in the middle of the Old Town.

Zamosc
$$$Hetmanska, ul. Staszica 7. Good house specialities.

Zakopane
$$Wierchy, Tetmajera 2, **$$Olbrachtowka**, Kraszewskiego 10, **$$U Wnuka**, Koscieliska 8. Three good restaurants for regional food.

Wroclaw
In addition to the hotel restaurants, the **$$$Krolewska**, Rynek 4, deserves special mention, but is not cheap.

Gniezno
$Gwarna, ul. Boleslawa Chrobrego 39. Good regional cuisine.

Poznan
$$$Hacjenda, ul. Moreasko 38, tel: 061-125278. On the northern outskirts of the city, concentrating in spite of its name on old Polish specialities. **$$Adria**, ul. Glogowska 14. Popular with tourists and trade fair visitors.

Fresh bread in Zakopane

Active Holidays

Sailing in Masuria

Windsurfing in the Baltic

Water sports

Poland has a wide range of sports facilities. The Baltic coast is ideal for water sport fans in particular. There are numerous beaches suitable for bathing, even though some sections (especially in the Gulf of Gdansk) are no-go areas due to the pollution level.

Those who prefer to swim or sail in fresh water have the thousand lakes of Masuria and the Pomeranian lake district to choose from. Windsurfing has also become increasingly popular. On the Masurian lakes windsurfers are still rather exotic and are obliged to share the water with numerous canoeists.

The numerous lakes in idyllic settings are often linked by rivers and canals, so that canoe tours of several days' duration can be planned. This is also facilitated by the fact that the most attractive lake shores have bivouac places for overnight stops in the midst of nature. The most beautiful river to canoe on is the 200-km (124-mile) Krutynia route, which winds its way through glorious countryside. The river is well supplied with bars, canteens, landing stages, bivouac grounds and water sports equipment is available to rent. Information: Polish Canoe Association: Polski Zwiazek Kajakowy, ul. Sienkiewicza 12/14, 00 010 Warsaw, tel: 022 27 49 16.

Fishing

The angling season in Poland lasts all year round and the abundant supply of fish in the rivers is attracting increasing numbers of anglers. Brown and rainbow trout are plentiful in the mountain rivers of Pomerania and the Masurian Lake District a paradise for flyfishers. In the Masurian lakes fishing with bait is allowed for catching pike, perch and catfish. The fighting barbels can be fished in the lower courses of the Pomeranian mountains, while abound in the fast waters of southern Poland.

Many Polish angling shops offer equipment at uncompetitively low prices but visitors need a licence to fish. During the summer season boat companies in the coastal resorts offer deep-sea fishing excursions. The Polish Angling Association (PAA) is at ul. Twarda 42, Warsaw, tel: 205083, and it has branches all over the country.

Cycling near the coast

Cycling

Poland is the ideal country for cyclists. Masuria is a popular destination, even though some of it is hilly, and the coastal region is also suitable for cycle tours. Quiet side roads, which are usually asphalted, are perfect for cyclists, but main roads should be avoided; there are no cycle paths in Poland.

Hikers in the Tatra Mountains

Horse riding

Poland had one of the greatest cavalry traditions in the world, and horses still work on the land. Arab breeding is an important export industry. There are numerous riding centres and state-owned stud farms offering 'Holidays in the saddle', with possibilities ranging from a day's riding to longer stays with accommodation, riding lessons are also available. The addresses of the centres can be obtained from the Polish Equestrian Sports Association: Polski Zwiazek Jezdziecki, ul. Sienkiewicza 12/14, 00 101 Warsaw, tel; 0048 22 27 01 97.

Climbing

The Sudety Mountains and the Carpathians provide many opportunities for mountain climbing. In the Tatra Mountains there are numerous climbing routes, involving a combination of mountain hiking and actual climbing. In recent years a well-signposted network of trails has also been laid out in Sudety. In the Tatra Mountains climbers who do not know the area should not embark on proper climbing tours without a guide.

Skiing

In winter the Tatra Mountains, which have an alpine character, have plenty to offer skiing enthusiasts, whether it be downhill or cross-country skiing and they are covered with snow from December through to March; in its highest areas, the snow remains until May. The winter sports mecca is Zakopane, which calls itself Poland's Winter Capital. The Sudety Mountains with their idyllic winter sports resorts and Szczyrk in the Silesian Beskid Mountains are also very attractive. The cross-country tracks in the Olsztyn area are now well-known, especially as snow is guaranteed in the winter months. There is also snow in Masuria, offering good cross-country skiing.

Poland has plenty to offer skiers

TRAMWAJE
WARSZAWSKIE

Getting There

Opposite: getting around Warsaw

By air

Most of the regular international flights land at Warsaw where a new terminal was opened in 1992 to handle the increasing number of passengers both with LOT, the Polish airline, and international carriers. International flights can also land at Cracow, Gdansk, Katowice, Posnan, Rzeszow and Szczecin. There are regular non-stop flights from London, New York, Chicago and Montreal. The flight time from the UK to Poland is approximately 2½ hours.

In the UK: Lot Polish Airlines, 313 Regent Street, London W1, tel: 0171-3230774.

In the US: Lot Polish Airlines, 500 Fifth Avenue, Suite 408, New York NY 10036, tel: 212-869 1074; 333 North Michigan Avenue, Suite 916, Chicago, IL 60601, tel: 312-236 3388/5501.

The new terminal, Warsaw

By sea

A weekly service is operated by the *M/S Inowroclaw*, a freighter carrying passengers from Felixstowe on a Monday and arriving in Gdynia of Fridays by way of Copenhagen. The journey time is approximately four days. For details, contact The Gdynia America Shipping Lines (London) Ltd, Passenger Department, 238 City Road, London EC1V 2QL, tel: 0171-251 3389.

Docking at Gdynia

By rail

There are international rail links between Poland and neighbouring European countries; from London a daily service runs from Liverpool Street Station via the Hook of Holland, to Poznan and Warsaw, and Victoria Station via Ostend and takes around 32 hours.

In the UK: British Rail International Enquiries, International Rail Centre, Victoria Station, London SW1, tel: 0171-834 2345.

In the US: Raileurope Inc. toll free on 1-800-4-EURAIL.

By coach

The cheap international buses to Poland are becoming an increasingly popular alternative to the train. The weekly services are run for most of the year in luxury, air-conditioned coaches. The Poland Express goes either from London via Amsterdam to Poznan and Warsaw; or from London or Manchester/Birmingham to Wroclaw, Katowice and Cracow. The journey takes about 30 hours. Contact your local travel agent for details.

By car

From the Hook of Holland or Ostend, the driving time to the Polish border is about 20 hours. Motorists should be in possession of an international driving licence, car registration documents and Green Card.

Trams crossing in Cracow

Getting Around

By air

Lot, the Polish national airlines has routes to 11 cities and towns. Book through Orbis travel agents.

By bus

In Poland there is a well-developed network of bus routes. All the large Polish towns have good public transport systems, consisting of trams, buses and trolleybuses, and it is therefore possible to reach most of the sights in this way. The tickets can be bought at kiosks (Kiosk Ruch), some shops and sometimes from the bus driver. A new ticket is required with every transfer but in some towns 10-fare tickets can be bought. In Warsaw one-day and weekly passes are available. You must stamp your ticket yourself when you get on the bus or tram. From 11pm the night rates come into force, which is double the usual fare.

By rail

To explore Poland by rail, the Polrail Pass entitles you to unlimited use of all Polish trains within a certain period with no limit to the distance travelled. This can be obtained in Poland or in Britain through British Rail International (*see page* 87).

By car

There are now petrol stations with unleaded petrol all over the country. The speed limit in built-up areas is 60 kph (37 mph) and outside built-up areas 90 kph (56 mph): on expressways it is 110 kph (68 mph). Seat belts are mandatory. In autumn and winter dipped headlights are required all day. Cars on roundabouts have right of way, so do all trams. A green arrow at the traffic lights indicates that right turns are permitted even when the lights are red – pedestrians beware.

Car hire

The big car rental firms operate through Rent-a-Car, Orbis and the Municipal Cab Company, so you can rent a car at any time at border crossings, airports, hotels, railway stations and some travel bureaux. To rent a car, you must be at least 21, be in possession of a valid passport, visa (if necessary) and international driver's licence.

On the road

Hitch-hiking

This is allowed in Poland as long as you buy a hitch-hikers book with 2,000km-worth of coupons. These are available from 'It' tourist information centres and branches of the Polish Society of Youth Hostels (PTSM). The hitch-hiking season runs from May to September.

Coachmen in Zakopane

Facts for the Visitor

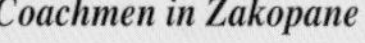

Travel documents

British visitors can stay in Poland for six months without a visa. Passport holders from most European countries, the US and the Commonwealth can stay for up to 90 days without a visa. Visitors are obliged to register their stay within 48 hours after crossing the border, which can be done at the hotel or campsite where you are staying.

Every foreign visitor who wishes to stay more than 90 days in Poland should report to the registration office in the nearest major town for a visa or extension of one.

Loss or theft of a passport should be reported at once to the consulate of the country which issued it in order to receive a substitute travel document.

Tourist information office

Tourist information

Most places will have one of the numerous tourist information offices with the 'IT' logo. They are usually run by the local Orbis offices and the Polish Tourist Association (PTTK). There are also IT desks in large hotels providing comprehensive information for visitors. To obtain information about Poland before you set out, contact:

In the UK: Polorbis, 82 Mortimer St, London W1N 7DE, tel: 0171-637 4971.

In the US: Orbis, 333 North Michigan Ave, Chicago, IL 60601, tel: 312-236 9013; Orbis, 500 Fifth Ave, Suite 1428, New York, NY 10036 (tel: 212-391 0844).

Child amusements

In Poland: Warsaw, Pl. Zamkowy 1/13, tel: 635-1881; **Cracow**, Ul. Pawia 8, tel: 226091, fax: 220471; **Gdansk**, Ul. Heweliusza 27, tel: 314355/ 316637; **Szczecin**, Ul. Wyszynskiego 26, tel: 340440; **Zakopane**, ul. Kosciuszki 23, tel: 12211, 66051; **Wroclaw**, Rynek 38, tel: 443111, fax: 442962; **Poznan**, Stary Rynek 59, tel: 526156.

Avoid the black market

Currency and exchange

Since 1995 Poland has two currencies: the old zloty and the new zloty. On 1 January the long-awaited *denominacja* was implemented, when the last four noughts were struck off the new banknotes. Now both currencies are equally valid. While the old zloty is still in circulation – and it is expected that it will be used until about 1997 – the chaos will be increased rather than reduced.

There is no longer a black market since the restrictions on currency exchange have been lifted. However, some of the old black market dealers have adapted to the changing circumstances: if a particularly favourable rate of exchange is offered to you on the street, don't accept it. The 'money changers' have been known to exchange with forged zloty notes or change large notes into small worthless ones by sleight of hand.

As well as banks there are numerous private exchange offices (kantors). Eurocheques are not accepted by all exchange offices and it may be necessary to go to a bank. The highest amount for which you can write a Eurocheque is 600 new zloty. Traveller's cheques are difficult to exchange even in large banks; credit cards are not yet accepted everywhere, but are taken by all large hotels, the airline companies, car hire firms and to an increasing extent exclusive restaurants and shops.

Customs

The import and export of zloty is still prohibited. All foreign currencies may however be imported and exported without restriction. Tourists are in theory obliged to declare their currency when entering or leaving the country, but in practice this is no longer required.

There is no restriction on bringing in items for personal use or presents, so long as the quantity does not suggest that the intention is to sell them. EU regulations apply to Polish goods taken out of the country.

Car drivers can only take out 10 additional litres of petrol in their reserve can in addition to what they have in the tank.

A souvenir of your trip

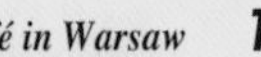

Café in Warsaw

Tipping

The price in restaurants includes a service charge. Here, however, as in all other relevant branches of the economy, such as taxis and hairdressers, tips at 10 percent are gladly received as a token of appreciation of good service.

Opening times

The opening times of shops, offices and museums vary quite considerably and are constantly changing but most businesses open weekdays 8am–7pm and generally close on Sundays.

Shops: In general it may be said that the larger the place, the more convenient the hours are for customers. Thus in every large town there is at least one grocery store that is open round the clock. Usually in the towns, shops are open on weekdays from 6am–6 or 7pm and 7am–1pm on Saturdays, closed Sundays and holidays.

In the country shops may close at 5pm, and markets run from 8am–7pm.

Banks: The private exchange offices are open until 6 or 7pm while the banks often only open their exchange counter from 10am to 1pm.

Post offices: Outside large towns post offices open from 8am–8pm. In the cities they are open 24 hours.

Restaurants: Those listed in *Food and Drink* usually open in the early afternoon and close at around 10pm.

Museums: Museums are usually closed on Monday (some also on Tuesday). From October to the end of April, they generally close earlier in the day. It is best to ask about opening hours beforehand at a tourist information office ('IT').The opening times of the different authorities vary, but in general their offices are open only in the morning.

Matrushka dolls

Public holidays

In addition to 3 May (Constitution Day in honour of the constitution of 1791), the public holidays are New Year's Day, Easter Monday, 1 May, Corpus Christi, Assumption Day (15 August), All Souls Day (1 November) and the two days at Christmas (25 and 26 December). Good Friday and Whit Monday are not official public holidays.

The 22 July holiday marking the founding of Communist Poland was dropped and replaced by 11 November marking the resurrection of the Polish State in November 1918.

Selling pretzels in Cracow

Postal services

The Polish postal and telecommunications service is still somewhat inadequate in spite of the numerous improvements that have been made. Letterboxes are usually red, the green boxes are for local letters only and the blue for airmail letters. Stamps are sold at post offices, which are usually open from 8am to 8pm, and also at many IT kiosks and hotels where postcards are also sold. The cost of stamps for letters and cards abroad is always going up as a result of inflation: ask at the post office or hotel reception what the current rates are.

Use the correct box

Telephone

Public telephone booths are either card phones or phones for which special tokens (*jetons*) are required. By contrast with the hopeless token-operated telephones, the new card telephones (the cards are available from post offices) are

Cardphones are the most efficient

easy to use. There are still places which do not have direct dialling facilities, but where the call has to be placed through the operator (code for the UK: 0044, for the States: 001). It is sometimes difficult to get a line to Poland from another country (code for Poland: 0048). AT&T: 010 480 0111; MCI: 010 480 0222. If outside Warsaw, first dial zero and wait for the second tone.

Newspapers and radio

The Times, *International Herald Tribune*, *Time* and *Newsweek* can be obtained in major cities on newsstands in hotels and some grocery stores. *Warsaw Voice*, a publication in English, is available not just in the capital but also in major tourist centres. This is aimed particularly at foreign visitors and includes numerous up-to-date tourist tips. For those with an interest in politics, there is a publication of news articles translated into English called the *Inside*.

The established Polish stations follow the old Eastern European tradition and broadcast outside the Western European frequency range of 66–73MHz. Conversion to Western European standards is currently in progress, and new frequencies will then also be available for the increasing number of private radio stations.

Guarded parking

Souvenir hunting in Zakopane

Security

The social changes, the decline of traditional values and the chaotic state of the police force created out of the hated militia seems to have caused an increase in crime since the early 1990s. It is still advisable to keep an eye on your belongings, especially in the big cities. This applies particularly to car drivers, whose Western deluxe vehicles are coveted most by the criminal element. The chances of getting your car back are small, and the stolen property generally disappears for good across Poland's eastern borders. Always make sure park your car in supervised car parks and ensure that you have adequate insurance for luggage as well.

Time

Central European time is used in Poland which is one hour forward from Greenwich Mean Time. Daylight saving time is applied from May through to September when the time is moved forward an hour.

Souvenirs

The choice of souvenirs to take home from Poland will depend primarily on the region in which you spend your holiday. On the Baltic coast, for example, by far the most popular souvenir is amber, either in its natural state or as jewellery, while in the Karkonosze it is lead crystal. Modern art or examples of traditional handicrafts (wood carvings, embroidered mats, pottery) also make an attractive present or memento. Good quality craft articles are available from the CEPELIA shops (eg in Old Town Square in Warsaw).

When buying at markets it is always a good idea to compare prices and to bargain. Collectors of nostalgic or unusual items can still find bargains at the numerous flea markets. However, no articles which were made before 1945 can be taken out of the country without the permission of the local preservation office.

Winter woollens

Voltage

Electricity is 220V. In accordance with the continental European norm, round two-pin plugs are used. Remember to bring an adaptor.

Medical

Visitors can get medical attention in any city clinic. Treatments and hospital stays must be paid for in foreign currency. Medications prescribed by Polish doctors may be paid for in zlotys. A travel insurance policy covering medical problems taken out before you travel is strongly recommended.

There is a good range of subsidised basic medicines available at very low prices in pharmacies, but most special medication is not stocked and has to be ordered, which takes time. It is therefore essential to take with you any medication on which you are reliant.

Pharmacies are open during normal business hours. In case of an emergency the addresses of the closest chemists on night duty are posted in the window.

Emergencies

Ambulance: tel: 999
Police: tel: 997
Fire: tel: 998

Dial 997 for police

Photography

Films and photographic material of well-known makes are available at prices comparable to those in the West; it may however be difficult to find slide films in smaller places. The larger towns have photo laboratories which can process your holiday photos in an hour.

Diplomatic representation

United Kingdom: aleja Roz 1, Warsaw, tel: 628-1001
United States of America: aleja Ujazdowskie 29, Warsaw, tel: 628-3041.
US Consulates: ul. Stolarska 9, Cracow, tel: 227793; ul. Chopina 4, Poznan, tel: 529586.

Accommodation

A wide range of accommodation is available for visitors to Poland from luxury Western-style hotels to camp sites in beautiful, remote areas. In the height of the season everywhere gets very booked up, so it is a good idea to reserve beforehand.

Hotels

Luxury hotels provide western standards at corresponding prices and belong to the international hotel chains such as Intercontinental, Marriott, Novotel and Forte. Some hotels of Poland's former monopoly enterprise Orbis have been privatised and modernised with foreign capital, but others are still waiting for the necessary renovation.

The prices of an overnight stay vary considerably and also differ according to the season and length of stay. The system of classification by stars is also rather confusing: many luxury hotels have voluntarily downgraded themselves in response to the graduated value-added tax introduced in 1994. The level of this tax depends on the 'degree of luxury' of the goods and services, ranging from 0 percent to 25 percent.

Holiday apartments

Inns and motels can be found along important main roads and many of them have a regional flavour.

Pensions are the equivalent to the British B&B and are located in popular tourist spots. Rooms can be reserved through tourist agencies.

In addition to hotels and pensions, small, privately-run boarding houses have begun to spring up in popular tourist spots. They are recommended for a real flavour of Polish hospitality and can also be reserved through tourist agencies.

Camping

Poland is a paradise for campers, with hundreds of camp sites for overnight stays in the midst of nature. Camp sites come in three categories and are usually open from 15 May to 15 September. Many have simply-furnished chalets, too. To make a camp site reservation, contact the agency Camptour, ul. Grochowska 331, 03 823 Warsaw, tel: 106050.

Ice cream Sunday

Hostels

In addition to the youth hostels, which are open all the year round, there are also seasonal youth hostels open just in the summer. An international youth hostel card entitles you to a 25 percent reduction. Although the hostels are in principle open to all age groups, preference is given to those under 26. Book four weeks in advance.

Polish Youth Hostels Association (PTSM), ul. Chocimska 28, 00 791 Warsaw, tel: 498128.

Hotel selection

The following are suggestions for Poland's main cities, listed according to the following categories: **$$$** (expensive); **$$** (moderate); **$** (inexpensive).

Cracow

$$$Forum, ul. Konopnickiej 28, tel: 669500, fax: 665827, modern hotel overlooking Wawel Hill. **$$$Francuski**, ul. Pijarska 13, tel: 225122, fax: 225270, a comfortable, traditional hotel restored in all its former glory. **$$$Grand**, ul. Slawkowska 5/7, tel: 217255, fax: 218360, the most famous hotel in Cracow. **$$Demel**, ul. Glowackiego 22, tel 361600; fax: 364543, very friendly service

Gdansk

$$$Hevelius, ul. Heweliusza 22, tel: 315631, fax: 311922. **$$$Marina**, ul. Jelitkowska 20, tel: 532079, fax: 530460. **$$$Posejdon** in the Jelitkowo district, 12 km (8 miles) from the city centre, ul. Kapliczna 30, tel: 531803, fax: 530228. All hotels are of a high standard. **$Jantar**, ul. Dlugi Targ 19, tel: 319532. Right on the Long Market.

Poznan

$$$Park, ul. Majakowskiego 77, tel: 41654, fax: 773830, scenically located on Lake Maltanskie, 3km (1¾ miles) from the city centre, the most modern hotel in Poznan.

Hotel in Poznan

Szczecin

$$$Radisson, pl. Rodla 10, tel: 595595, fax: 594594 – the best and most modern hotel in the city. **$$$Neptun**, ul. Matejki 18, tel: 240111, fax: 225701, has all the comforts of a first-class hotel. Both hotels are located in the city centre.

Warsaw

$$$Bristol, ul. Krakowskie Przedmiescie 42/44, tel: 625 2525, fax: 625 2577. **$$$Marriott**, al. Jerozolimskie 65/79, tel: 630 6306, fax: 300050. **$$$Victoria Intercontinental**, ul. Krolewska 11, tel: 279271, fax: 279856. **$$Jan III Sobieski**, pl. Zawiszy 1, tel: 658 4444, fax: 659 3828. **$$Cytadela**, Krajewskiego 3, tel: 687 7236. **$Dom Turysty Harenda**, ul. Krakowskie Przedmiescie 4/6, tel: 260071, fax: 262625. Inexpensive rooms in the centre.

A friendly welcome

Wroclaw

$$$Wroclaw, ul. Powstancow Slaskich 7, tel: 614651, fax: 616617, in the city centre, has a swimming pool, sauna and solarium and facilities for the disabled. **$$Monopol**, ul. Modrzejewskiej 2, tel: 37041, fax: 448033, one of the oldest luxury hotels in Poland, with more outward show than comfort.

Index